Hierarchy and Free Expression in the Fight against Racism

Denis G. Rancourt

With an introduction by
Mahdi Darius Nazemroaya

ISBN 978-0-9859942-8-0

STAIRWAY≡PRESS

www.stairwaypress.com
1500A East College Way #554
Mount Vernon, WA 98273

Cover Design by Guy Corp, www.grafixCORP.com

Contents

Hierarchy and Free Expression in the Fight Against Racism

Identifying Racism: Context of Rancourt's Critique—Introduction by Mahdi Darius Nazemroaya

Why an Introduction by Me?

CRITICIZING ANTI-RACISM has been somewhat of a taboo, even if the criticism is constructive. If we have taboos restricting dialogue on important subjects, how can we address and understand the relevant issues? This book seeks to break these taboos and cross several barriers in addressing anti-racism. Its author, Denis G. Rancourt, has not been one to shy away from controversy or controversial subjects.

In the years that I have known him, controversy after controversy has followed Denis. The storm clouds have never been far behind him: his highly popular university activism course, which he opened to all members of the community; his embrace of critical pedagogy to democratize university classrooms; his A+ marking scheme purportedly used as a means to establishing a qualitative pass/fail marking system in his quantum physics and solid state mechanics courses; his longstanding dispute over academic freedom with the bureaucracy at the University of Ottawa, starting with Gilles G. Patry and then his successor Liberal Party of Canada heavyweight and former federal cabinet minister, Allan Rock; his climate change essay, which was supported by York University historian David F. Noble, that challenged the consensus on global warming while receiving wide attention amongst critics of anthropogenic global warming, including U.S. Senator James Inhofe; and his *U of O Watch* blog, dedicated to exposing "institutional corruption" at his own institute, have all put him straight in the line of fire. There is no other way to say it, except that the man is notorious for ruffling a lot of feathers and creating "cognitive dissonance." He is a true gadfly, but a determined one who will not drink the hemlock or go away. He and I have not always seen things eye to eye, but I have always respected him for boldly and passionately speaking his mind and expressing his ideas freely and trying to put them into practice.

Sometimes I think of Rancourt as an outlander or traveler looking at society from an outside view, but then I realize that he is not detached and is actually writing in a deliberately attached way from the inside. One can actually sense that his writing is a metabolic reaction and that the man is screaming sometimes through his essays, asking us to please open our eyes and take a look at the world around us and the state of affairs society is inundated in. I cannot help but think of how Bell Hooks described this process; for her, speaking and writing her views and ideas was a way to carry out a process of "active self-transformation and a rite of passage" that allowed her to become a subject instead of remaining an object with no agency. Rancourt's essays throughout the years have also been part of his own praxis and movement as a social actor. They are not some academic production, but a reflective thought process that has been transparently laid out for us. Nor is he caught in the trap of thinking his work will change the world; he has written with the hope that committed individuals will reflect on his ideas and proposals while developing their own praxes.

The Rancourt that I know is not the one that is distinguished in the scientific community for his leading research on Mössbauer spectroscopy or for finding the theoretical solution about the Invar alloy's thermal expansion anomaly and his discovery of the phenomenon of superferromagnetism, but the one known as a social thinker. Reviewing his writing and exchanging ideas with him over the years has always proved to be rewarding. As a sociologist who is familiar with a lot of the underlying aspects it encompasses, I readily agreed when Denis approached me to write the foreword for his book on anti-racism. Eventually the foreword I agreed to write for him transformed itself into a complementary introduction for his book as I immersed myself in his manuscript and had repeated exchanges with him about his ideas. Although our two styles are visibly different, this introduction sets the tempo for the topics Rancourt will be tackling.

There are also added dimensions of personal relevance about the subjects of racism and anti-racism for me. Although a relatively young nation, Canada is not without a long history of racism. Most Canadians casually recognize and acknowledge this when they are reminded about the unjustifiable mistreatment of the Aboriginals, the maltreatment of Chinese workers, the prejudiced laws against Asians, the exploitation of Eastern European immigrants, the cleavages between Anglophone Canada and Francophone Canada, the disastrous Indian residential school system, the war time internment and removal of the citizenship of Japanese-Canadians (including those of German, Austrian, and Magyar/Hungarian background), the Russophobe attitudes against Soviet citizens and Russians during the Cold War, Canada's segregation policies, the displacement of the "black" residents of Africville in Nova Scotia, and so on. Jews and Muslims have suffered too, albeit these two groups are not races and it is incorrect to place either one of them in racial categories as is so often done. We have also had a long and tense history of discrimination by the Protestant and Roman Catholic communities against one another in Canada.

The legacy of the systemic oppression of Aboriginal Canadians has scarred the First Nations, Inuit, and Métis and continues until this day in Canada. Even the United Nation's Committees on the

Elimination of Racial Discrimination and the Rights of the Child have criticized Canada about the condition of Aboriginals. From a personal perspective, I remember the lingering and conditioned Russophobe attitudes that were generally still present amongst members of the Canadian military when I was serving as a young soldier, not to mention the misconceptions of other soldiers about the Arabs, the Chinese, Islam, and the entire continent of Africa. Canadians that are practicing Islam have been called "Canadian-born Muslims" (meaning they are born in Canada, but are not Canadian) through alienating selective language used by the media and Muslim women regular face discrimination; at the time of this writing I was told by a young Muslim girl working in one of Ottawa's main hospitals that about once or twice a week she is insulted or turned away by patients while she is doing her job merely as a result of her hijab or head scarf. Year after year, Public Safety Canada continuously reports that Canadian jails have a disproportionate number of minorities, like Canada's Aboriginals. Racism and prejudice are not only a part of the history of Canada, but intertwined in different ways in the very social fabrics of Canadian society.

Aside from being a sociologist, I have additionally found discussion about the subject of racism of personal relevance as someone who can be categorized as a minority. Personally befriending notable societal actors such as Reverend Walter E. Fauntroy, one of the leaders of the African-American Civil Rights Movement and the envoy of Martin Luther King, Jr. to U.S. Presidents John F. Kennedy and Lyndon Johnson at the White House, has also honed my interests on the subject. Hearing the stories of people like Walter about their struggles and experiences against racism while spending important moments together has enforced this. Moreover, I was exposed to critical discussions on the subject of anti-racism at an early point in my life. My former high school science teacher and friend Roger Taguchi—a gifted intellectual who worked on his chemistry doctorate under the supervision of Noble Prize laureate John Polanyi, who was recognized as one of the province of Ontario's best teacher in 2000, and who won Carleton University's High School Teaching Award in 2003—had questioned the effectiveness of anti-racism policies. As a Japanese-Canadian whose family had suffered from racism in Canada during the Second World War, Roger had a good grasp of the subject and was one of the first people I heard criticizing certain anti-racism policies as counter-productive. He did not like the mentality of "victimhood" that was conditioned into certain minorities, which he saw as psychologically and socially harmful.

Reform versus Revolution

During my own moments of reflection on Rancourt's ideas, I could not resist thinking back to the collision of ideas that existed between the two giants of the African-American Civil Rights Movement in the 1960s, Baptist Christian minister Reverend Martin Luther King, Jr. and the Muslim leader Malcolm X. The ideas of both civil rights and community leaders clashed on how to establish equality and equity for the African-American population. Although their ultimate objectives to escape oppression were the same, King and Malcolm X advocated for different methods for African-Americans. Malcolm X disapproved of the former's "passive resistance" position saying that the oppressed had a natural right to fight back "actively" as a form of defence. Because he was teaching them not to fight the "white man" while African-Americans were fighting amongst themselves, Dr. King was disarming "blacks" in the eyes of Malcolm X and his followers. From Malcolm's view this was why Martin Luther King, Jr. had the support of members of the dominant "white" class. According to the journalist and author Max Wallace, King was even afraid to initially oppose the Vietnam War, because he thought it could alienate the Johnson Administration; only after the African-American boxing icon Muhammad Ali refused to publicly support the war did King voice his opposition. On the other hand Dr. King preached for patience, dialogue, and the use of the "weapons of love" hoping that the oppressive "whites" would become cognizant that they were supporting injustice. The major difference we have between the viewpoints among these two great protagonists of the African-American Civil Rights Movement is that one is calling for societal reform, while the other for a path towards revolution. Additionally, some would argue that the significant difference between Malcolm X and King was not so much that one was a revolutionary and the other was a reformist, but rather that King was pursuing civil rights for African-Americans with a view to integrating them into American society on the same basis as "whites" (as individuals), while Malcolm X was pursuing self-determination for African-Americans as a culturally distinct people in pursuit of a common collective future.

An important point has to be made here about the clashes between ideas of reform versus revolution. The old system of privileges based on social inequalities that are tied to the existing hierarchy in society, in whatever shape they take place and form, can potentially exist—even thrive—under a new social order brought about by reforms. While apartheid was politically removed in South Africa, for example, the economic unequal relationships it sustained have mostly remained intact and have even been exported under a thriving economic model to neighbouring African countries, such as Mozambique.

In the case of Dr. King and Malcolm X, the dominant class could live with the former's view of a reformed social order, but could not tolerate the latter's view of revolution that would create a totally new social order. What can be described as the most radical or militant of African-American activists would adamantly contend that African-Americans serving as U.S. officials like Secretary of State Condoleezza Rice, General Colin Powell, and Ambassador Susan Rice all serve the interests of the dominant "white" class in the United States as subservient "Uncle Toms." In summary, the argument is that power and hegemonic relationships take advantage of reforms. Unlike revolutionary spaces, they find niches for themselves in "reformed" social, political, and economic spaces and seek to maintain the core of the old social order under a cosmetic facelift.

Although this debate is being outlined in a binary of black and white (no play on words or pun intended), it should be noted that there are in many instances middle paths and grey regions between the two sides. Yet, it should also be mentioned that any old social order of power and hegemonic relationships can be very resilient, flexible, and elastic; these forces can quickly advance into the grey space between social reform and revolution and colonize it like an invading bacterial growth resettling lost space. In the People's Republic of China this is exactly what happened to spur the process of capitalist restoration under communism. Capitalist restoration unfolded in mainland China, because of the leeway given to the "patriotic bourgeois" or capitalist class by the Communist Party of China, which even accepted members of the capitalist class into its ranks. This social reform versus revolution is relevant also in discussing critical race theory.

Pushing the Limits of the Academy

Denis Rancourt's thoughts distinguish him as one of Canada's most challenging cultural critics. In regard to social relations, his arguments lean towards the revolutionary ideas of Malcolm X and the radicals; he is not a reformer. His description of himself would be as someone who believes in "reform via revolutionary sparks, rather than via gradual progress." In all his writing, including this book, Denis works to question the social contract and the inner watch tower inside the individual that keeps him or her in place within the contours of their societal scripts as social conformists.

On a parallel track, he has made a lot of the same conclusions that other social theorists have, but the British scholar Paul Gilroy of the London School of Economics and Political Science is the one that most prominently comes to mind. While Gilroy's work has spoken more about class struggle, Denis has spoken more by way of an analysis of hierarchy. Both Gilroy and Rancourt, however, are travelers on the same intellectual road and both ultimately call for social emancipation from the oppressive forces that control society.

Even if you do not agree with Rancourt's ideas, his arguments will cognitively enrich you. In addition, a bit of skepticism is healthy. Debates are worth having and his arguments serve as good starting points for vigorous exchanges. His points of view are not easily dismissed. Rancourt gives readers a new set of glasses to see the world and his reference to racism as part of a broader biological, psychological, and social or bio-psycho-social mechanism brings a fresh outlook into the arena of debate. Walking a fine line, Rancourt actually wants us to recognize that racism (as a form of differentiating prejudice towards other groups) is a tool and part of our array of primal survival mechanisms linked to a group formation process. As an intellectual he has put forward excellent points for much needed reflection.

Nor has his work and writing style been immersed in jargon. Denis does not want to waste the reader's time or to use any unnecessary words or to make any type of superficial presentation. He writes in an inclusive language that seeks to remove barriers, so that laypersons and experts alike can read and make their own assessments about what he is saying. His writing serves to mentally provoke his readers to think and to consider or reconsider their standpoints. Ultimately, Rancourt's aims are to break taboos and to show a crystallized view that in the mainstream we have been detached, like zombies, and muzzled from questioning many of the relationships we take for granted.

How a researcher, physicist, environmental scientist, bio-geo-chemist, and dissident tenured professor such as Denis Rancourt has crossed into the realm of cultural study, should come as no surprise to those familiar with him. Nor should the legitimacy of his crossover be questioned on the basis of academic segregation. There are no real limits and boundaries between disciplines. In the bigger and much clearer scheme of things the divisions between the disciplines are really arbitrary forms of categorization. Any limits dividing the study of chemistry from the studies of physics and geoscience or the study of political science from the studies of anthropology, sociology, criminology, and economics are constructed barriers. Likewise, the barriers between the natural sciences and social sciences are constructed barriers. Outside of the institutional confinements of the academy there are no monopolies and restriction on the fields of analyses, knowledge, and inquiry. To place such barriers and enforce such distinctions is a form of classism. Knowledge is a unitary body, even if interest, perception, categorization, and possession of knowledge are not.

Rancourt is not alone in his interdisciplinary path either. The U.S. intellectual Noam Chomsky is a linguist, but that has not stopped him from being a well-known voice on social issues. Chomsky's friend, the Belgian physicist Jean Bricmont at the Université catholique de Louvai (UCL) also crossed over into the social sciences long ago. Edward O. Wilson is a biologist, but that never stopped him from venturing into the field of philosophy and giving rise to sociobiology. The British anthropologist Alfred Haddon was originally a biologist and zoologist. Maximilian Weber, one of the central figures of modern sociology, was a lawyer. Avicenna, the Samanid author of the encyclopedic *Canon of Medicine* that forms the basis of modern medicine, crossed into the field of medical practice from mathematics, philosophy, and metaphysics. Zachariah Razi, another great physician, was also another polymath who followed a similar path as Avicenna. Copernicus, the Polish astronomer who popularized the heliocentric model of the solar system, was a Roman Catholic jurist and cleric.

Rancourt's belief that specialized fields of science cannot be divided from politics and the daily affairs of people led him down this road of multiple disciplines. He would not voluntarily alienate himself or silence his voice about political, sociological, and economic issues. This is why Denis has not hesitated to cross into territory that has been delineated as an arena for the social sciences. This rationale was also part of the raison d'être for the creation of his student-directed science and society course in the Faculty of Science at the University of Ottawa, a course which was never allowed to run again after it filled the largest auditorium on campus.

Compartmentalized and atomized research is a form of intellectual alienation. The best way I can think of explaining this is by giving the example of certain forms of weapons manufacturing and research which are broken up and divided amongst different individuals and groups; that way the individuals are all alienated from the weapon and not conscious of what their work really entails, the destructive nature of their product. Knowledge can also be appropriated and exploited like this and individuals are distanced from their tasks and any notions of social responsibility in what they do. The constructed fields and disciplines and their practitioners in our modern academies are integral components of this "political process." I think that if there is anything to be learned and extrapolated from the publication in 1962 of Thomas Kuhn's *The Structure of Scientific Revolutions*, it is that science in its institutionalized form and its paradigm shifts are not only prone to the effects of the subjectivity of the scientific community, but that by extension they are tied to the political. Economists and political scientists do not merely serve to study and analyze economics and politics; they also serve to justify economic and political decisions and the societal status quo in many instances. The way this form of education and presentation of knowledge is packaged is as a disarming "apolitical" and neutral process, which makes indoctrination readily acceptable in the mainstream. Views that the modern academy is an "apolitical" institution are also incorrect and contrary to documented history.

All systems of power either appreciate, or, at a very minimum, tolerate the "apolitical," because under the mantle of neutralism it never challenges the status quo.

What Is Racism?

With little thought, most people would agree that no discussion of racism can start without discussing race and the subject of race relations or without at least establishing a basic understanding of race. It has to be pointed out, however, that an understanding of race alone is not enough for understanding the phenomenon of racism. Yet, before we move on to discuss race and the other elements tied to racism, a few words should be mentioned about the emergence of the study of racism in the social sciences and humanities.

Analyses of what used to be identified as race, as well as race relations, has experienced a shift towards the study and analyses of racism and racialization. Out of the two latter subjects, fewer inquiries have been made about racialization. While there is a wealth of literature on racism and the study of race in the social sciences and humanities, racialization is still a subject that needs greater study and discussion. Racialization by definition is the process of conceptualizing or constructing racial or ethno-cultural groups, as well as developing a *race consciousness* to enforce social distance, and is deeply tied to identity politics and in most understandings is a process tied to de-humanization. It is also tied to the construction of hierarchical *race orders*.

In this book, using a radical liberation perspective, an argument is also made about the utilization of racialization and the development of race consciousness by oppressed groups to identify a group of oppressors as a "race" as a means of combating them through a functionalist form of counter-racism. This is what Rancourt calls "up racism," which he refers to as a form of class struggle. A real life example of something like this process is in Africa during the de-colonization period after 1945 when this form of counter-racism against European colonial settlers actually took place. Justifiable or not, the example of radical feminists and their counter-sexism, which is a form of reverse sexism against males, can also be conceptualized as a comparison to this counter-racism.

14

Racism is based on what is considered an organized set of beliefs that are called racial prejudices which view certain ethnic or racial groups as either inferior or in negative terms in relations to other racial or ethnic groups. There are differences between what is considered to be ethnicity and what is considered to be race, but racism is applied to both of them in the same manner and thus we need not delve into the differentiation between the two concepts too much when speaking about the application of racism. All we need to know is that race is a term used to categorize specific groups of people on the basis of distinguishable physical characteristics and that ethnicity is a composite term anchored in both objective and subjective features of a group of people that can include identity, culture, language, and nationality.

Race is also the more rigid of the two concepts and there is an increasing trend in the disciplines of anthropology and sociology to phase out the term race and to replace it with ethnicity. The anthropologist Charles Loring Brace's book *"Race" is a Four-Letter Word* is an example of this migration away from the concept of race by anthropologists and sociologists on the basis of their "realization that there is no biological justification for the concept of 'race.'" Racism's definition in sociological terms is also more precise than just racial prejudice. Racism is the prejudiced beliefs about the innate inferiority of some ethnic or racial groups combined with the power to transform such ideas and beliefs into practices that can deny or exclude equality of treatment on the basis of ethnicity or race. This definition is important and lends credence to the central thesis of this book.

Racism has five typologies. These typologies are overt, polite, subliminal, institutional, and systemic racism. Overt racism, which is also referred to as "redneck racism" by some scholars, takes place in public and is unhidden. It is there for all to see. This is the easiest form of racism to address and combat. Polite racism on the other hand attempts to disguise racist attitudes and the dislike of other ethnic or racial groups. This type of racism has been widely studied in the workplace and includes subtle jokes, underhanded remarks, stereotypes, biased hiring practices, biased grading, and behaviour that acts to single out members of another group. Subliminal racism involves unconscious prejudice towards other groups. This form of racism is tied to ethnocentric views that most racist people are unaware of, because it has structurally been conditioned and socialized in them through societal forces like their culture, institutions, and media. The view that the turbans of Sikhs and head scarves of Muslim women are un-North American and alien is an example of this subliminal racism. These three categories of racism all exist at the individual, group, and societal levels; they also reflect cultural beliefs or individual beliefs shaped predominately by socio-cultural forces. Moreover, it is more than a legitimate question to ask if individual racism, which includes ethnocentrism, is a reflection of structural realities that prevail in a society.

While the first three forms of racism are acted out at the individual and societal levels, the next two categories are tied to group structures. Institutional racism is racism at the level of the state in which a society's laws, procedures, and practices directly and openly accept a racial hierarchy or prevent certain racial or ethnic groups, whether they are a minority or a majority, from having equal involvement, status, and rights in a society. Ethnocracies like Apartheidist South Africa and Portuguese West Africa (Angola) are examples of places with institutional racism. Systemic racism is caused by practices, rules, and procedures within an institution that have the consequences of discriminating against a specific group. What differentiates systemic racism from institutional racism is that systemic racism can be unintended or at least a claim can be made that it is unintended. This latter category of racism can additionally be compounded with institutional racism as institutional-systemic racism. Of course these five categories of racism that have been outlined can also overlap in various ways.

At a cultural and societal level of analysis, racism does not simply occur because an individual or a group naturally dislikes another group of people for innate and intrinsic reasons that are specific to that group. So to speak, there is a method behind the madness. For example, the German scholar Maximilian Weber explained the dislike and racial prejudices felt against Poles by German farmers was really a reflection of economic competition between them.

Two key points must now be made about the comprehensive sociological definition of racism that was outlined earlier. These points are vital to any discussion on racism and both involve the words "organized" and "power," which steer us towards power structures.

Firstly, the organized nature of racist beliefs, as part of an overarching matrix of prejudiced beliefs that include ageism and sexism, has a strong interplay with institutions and hierarchies in a society.

Secondly, the "power to transform these ideas into practice" denotes that power differentials are an integral component of racism. This again points us in the direction of what is ultimately a structure of hierarchy, which is fundamentally a stratified system of superiors and inferiors.

There are different types of hierarchies, such as patriarchies (societies controlled by men) and matriarchies (societies controlled by women), which are usually more sophisticated than a set of linear relationships. Although invisible, there are also hierarchies based on race, as argued by the Canadian sociologist John Porter's seminal work *The Vertical Mosaic: an Analysis of Social Class and Power in Canada*. This ethnic delineation has primed the American philosopher Charles W. Mills to declare that racism itself is actually a "political system" and "a particular power structure of formal or informal rule." Social scientists and political thinkers have made several widely accepted conclusions on the basis of such observations about the relationships between racism, class, economics, power, and hierarchy under different paradigms or distinct patterns of thought.

Different Perspectives for Analyzing Racism

From a functionalist perspective, it can be argued that racism serves to maintain a hierarchical system either by keeping groups in their places, dividing groups, keeping a social distance between groups, and distracting subordinate segments of society by scapegoating minorities or a particular group for all their problems. This essentially means discrimination is a form of hierarchical regulation that helps maintain the social status quo. Thus, prejudiced beliefs and negative attitudes are put into practice by the dominant group(s) and their representatives—the so-called "Uncle Toms" or "House Negros," which will be addressed later—against members of the subordinate group(s) as a form of regulation.

To the influential American sociologist Robert Park it was clear that *race relations*, as racism was referred to by scholars, were the product of migration, conquest, and colonization. For the sake of precision it has to be mentioned that subordinate groups are not necessarily racial either—they can be defined by sex, gender, occupation, lineage, tribe, nationality, caste, geography, or class. Structural-functionalists would also argue that racism is used to keep society stable by forcing cultural conformity and assimilation. Even a society's matrimonial preferences or preferences for monogamy, polygamy, polygyny, and polyandry are based on function and service and can be linked to racial prejudice. Homogamy, a pattern of matrimony or cohabitation in which individuals pair with others that have similar characteristics that can range from faith, ethnicity, ideology, age, nationality, class, and education, falls into line with the belief that society's want conformity and the belief that racism is actually a form of cultural and normative coercion.

From a structural-functionalist tradition it can also be argued that racism has forced the biological assimilation and cultural assimilation or acculturation of vast segments of indigenous peoples across the globe. Although Malcolm X would later change or qualify his views after returning from his second pilgrimage to Mecca,

Monthly Review featured an interview with him conducted by A.B. Spellman on March 19, 1964 where he argued that the integration of the already disenfranchised African-American population was a means to lure and co-opt them into the lower classes of society in the United States. In a January 1965 interview with Pierre Berton, Malcolm X would also point out that he was not hostile to integration per se or ethnic intermarriage, but it was the dominant "white" class that collectively was opposed to it as a means of maintaining the divisions in American society and the social distance between themselves and "non-whites." The key difference between Malcolm's two positions is that his earlier position called for separation, which has to be done voluntarily and by groups that are essentially equal, while the second position he describes is one where the dominant societal group imposes segregation, which is forced upon inferiors by superiors as a practice of power.

Marxist analysts and other conflict theorists would argue that these phenomena are tied to economic relationships and, in turn, economic relationships are the basis for the socio-economic class structures that shape the vast majority of societal hierarchies. Feminist analysis would tend to agree while adding sex and gender into the equation.

As hinted earlier, sexism also plays a similar function as racism, while gendered institutions and gender belief systems also serve to preserve societal hierarchies and power structures. Libertarian and anarchist perspectives would argue that at the core, it is the power structures, which the state and institutions represent, that have an interest in utilizing racism to maintain their controls and that a laissez-faire attitude and either de-centralization or the most direct and accessible forms of democracy are the only way to eliminate racism. State regulations and laws do not eliminate racism from the perspective of libertarians and anarchists, they entrench racism.

One theory from the conflict perspective, *racial formation theory*, maintains that the government plays a large part in defining ethnic relations and racialization. Although predominately statists, Marxists share similar views with libertarians and anarchists about the link between racism and those holding power in a society. Marxists, however, see racism as indicative of class conflict and would argue that capitalist elites controlling the state are the ones that institute racist policies to maintain their power and to divide the proletariats and other classes as part of a latent class war that the ruling classes are consciously waging against the unconscious lower classes.

Although they have been criticized for not analyzing social stratification in more depth, the interpretative or interactionist perspective and microsociology, particularly symbolic interactionism, put emphasis on ongoing individual interaction, meaning, agency, social location, and the shaping of perceptions as the basis for the development of racism. Ethnomethodologists, and their observational form of research, attempt to discover the ways that people make sense of the social world and the daily events in their lives; they would study how an individual becomes racist or is affected by racism through the interpretation of their experiences.

Dramaturgical analysis, which compares daily social life to a theatrical or dramatic presentation, interprets individual behaviour as a form of impression management in front of society (the audience) to act out what that individual believes is their social script; dramaturgy would look at the *front stage* idealized presentation of one's self and an individual's behaviour towards members of other groups, defined by social expectations and concepts of social roles and statuses, that an individual would present to their audience (society) when being watched versus their *back stage* attitudes and behaviour towards other groups when the audience (society) is not watching them.

Akin to all these interpretative views, phenomenologists believe that our social realities, including racist attitudes, are a product of our socially derived collective activities, which ultimately cannot be detached from individual subjectivity. These approaches all look at what is broadly referred to as the social construction of reality and its interplay with individual interpretation. This is one of the points where notions tied to socialization like the self-concept and personality developed by Charles Horton Cooley and George Herbert Mead can make one of their many entrances into the realm of analysis about racism.

Social constructionists agree with much of the above, but focus more in an outwardly direction of meaning. They maintain that people see their interactions as natural and argue that the concepts of race and "whiteness" and "blackness" are socially and politically constructed and defined as what are called *social constructs*. As Western European imperialism expanded around the world, the social construct of "whiteness" was expanded and adopted in conquered lands. Several different hierarchies of expanding "whiteness" also developed which slowly calibrated with one another and then absorbed the "off-whites" as capitalism fussed with their cultures and societies. While the Portuguese and Spaniards used their own definitions of "whiteness" to establish complex racial hierarchies in their colonies, they were portrayed as inferior and as "off-white" by the English and other Northern Europeans. This changed with time as the concept and polity of Europe expanded alongside a European race consciousness that was needed to create solidarity against the dominated peoples of the Third World. Soon the "off-whites" of Portugal, Spain, Italy, and Greece were "whitened" and brought into the racial fold. Similarly, there have been fluctuations in "whiteness" that have worked to exclude groups that were once considered "white" under some of the past hierarchies of "whiteness."

The recognition of the role of labeling practices on perception and behaviour by symbolic interactionists opens the door for an analysis that would accept the roles of power structures. Indeed, symbolic interactionists constantly assess how social structures and institutions affect individuals. Here we can make a leap from the interpretative perspective to larger scale analyses, specifically constructionist ones. This offers a segue for what the French social theorist Michel Foucault called *governmentality*, which can roughly be described as the way that governmental policies and state institutions deliberately shape or socialize people.

Although occurring on too grand a scale to be thought of as symbolic interaction at play, the bureaucratic Soviet and Chinese ethnicization—a term akin to racialization—policies in Central Asia that helped sculpt the identities and differences between various Turkic populations are an example of this governmentality process.

Symbolic interaction also takes hierarchy into account in its analyses of racism, because social structures shape who an individual interacts with and how they interact with them. Social psychologists, whether leaning more on the psychological or sociological sides, also examine racism through a symbolic interactionist perspective or *social structure and personality* perspective that would focus on the connections between the racist attitudes of individuals and societal conditions, specifically social structures. Aside from experience, stereotypes are additionally considered by those using an interpretive analysis of racism.

All these perspectives are different lenses of analysis that ultimately point in the same direction by looking for general patterns to formulate explanations through a study of the particular. Such theoretical perspectives or paradigms can be used like lenses to see things from different perspectives; this book represents another such lens, one that emphasizes the centrality of social tensions.

Although each has its nuances and irregularities, no matter how one identifies with these paradigms, they all try to sociologically make sense of racism. Most practitioners of these different perspectives would also agree that racism is a social construct. Historically, there has been an interface between groupings (which includes class) and ethnicity that fall into the matrix of hierarchical systems. As Porter argued in the case of Canadian society, Canada is a mosaic of different ethnic, linguistic, geographic, and religious groupings that are unequal in status and power. Although Porter tried to push away his work from a Marxian direction, what he revealed meant that Canadian society was divided into class groupings. Class itself creates (or is created by) a system of hierarchy, which is what libertarians and political anarchists alongside analysts from a conflict perspective denote as the basis of racism. We can conclude from all these different perspectives that racism, including its interplay with dominance and social statuses, can be viewed similarly to class conflict, if not as class conflict itself.

Anti-Racism and Critical Race Theory

Things are not always as they seem, especially in the worlds of political economy and sociological analysis. The aspect of the sociological definition of racism that involves power is usually overlooked by the vast majority of readers and practitioners, including anti-racism activists who merely focus on employment policies and cases of individual racism without focusing on the structural causes of racism. Although much of their work can be admirable and commendable, it really does not address the sources of racism. These anti-racism activists are actually civil rights watchdogs. True anti-racism work takes much more in-depth action. In many cases these civil rights watchdogs are not really reducing racism, but actually maintaining it in a locked state. Anti-racism can also take the shape of McCarthyism and be used to silence critical thinking and dissent. The Institute for the Study of Academic Racism (ISAR) is one body that has been accused of this.

Nor does formal equality before the law mean practical equality in society, if the socially structured basis of racism is left unaddressed. This can take a variety of forms. One example of how racism could remain is as follows: while racial equality and rights are entrenched politically and legally in a state's structure, racial equality is not socially accepted by the dominant culture; this means that racism will prevail and play out in voting habits, hiring practices, and even disregard for equality laws. The 1958 Notting Hill and 2011 London riots emerged precisely because of these political and cultural contradictions in England.

Most people, including people who call themselves anti-racism activists, fail to grasp the foundations and fundamentals of racism. Without an understanding of the role of power relationships any efforts to address racism and its causes will always come short. The important question that must be asked is as follows: why is it that the vast majority of people are not aware of the precise definition of racism, which includes power? This is one gap that this book has taken the task upon itself to fill and address from a critical perspective. It can be part of a process to revive or reclaim critical race theory in the tradition of the prominent British cultural studies expert Paul Gilroy.

Racial relations began to change after the end of the Second World War in 1945. De-colonization began to take root in all the colonies of Western Europe and the African-American and American Native communities began to clamour for their civil rights. In the world of theory and academia the discourse on race began to change and eventually catch up to events in the real world—it had no choice.

These real world events were the liberation movements and revolutions of what became the Third World, the African-American Civil Rights Movement and the American Indian Movement in the U.S., and Québécois and Aboriginal Canadian mobilization for greater rights in Canada. At about the same time the second-wave of the women's or feminist movement also began. In all these struggles the role of power was recognized as the basis of the racism and inequality used to justify subordination. Eventually, critical race theory was formed.

Critical race theory stipulates that race and racism have played critical roles in political and legal structures. The theory also stipulates that racism is such an engrained feature of North American society that it is invisible to people and that racist behaviour goes unnoticed to most people as ordinary behaviour. Central to critical race theory in North America is the belief that "white elites" or specifically White Anglo-Saxon Protestant (WASP) elites "tolerate"—an important word—and encourage racial advances in societal structures for non-WASPs and minorities on the basis of protecting their own group interests.

In other words, from the perspective of critical race theory, a "House Negro" is promoted to protect the dominant group's interests. This inter-racial alliance should make it clear that racial analysis has its limits and that an analysis of power structure needs to be made where racial analyses leave off. Any notion that there is a racial war between WASPs and non-WASPs, such as the Franco-Québécois or African-Americans, without realizing its function for maintaining a hierarchy of power, actually diverts one from the realization that racial prejudice and racial conflict are used to maintain a small group in power that also oppresses the majority of their own "race" too. These elites are not racist per se, they are elitist and want to maintain their powers and they are willing to collaborate with people from outside their group to do so, regardless of ethnicity, racial group, class, and so on. Moreover, many of the categories of people being dealt with in racial wars are all social constructs intended to de-politicize, disarm, or camouflage the political basis of racial conflicts.

Condemnation of racism—or what is presented as racism—is also selectively applied. This too is an issue of power. The way racism is perceived or looked at is not equal or balanced at all. In 1995, Québécois Premier Jacques Parizeau blamed what he called money and "the ethnic vote" when the sovereigntists or separatists in the province of Québec lost their second referendum to become an independent country. His remarks were heavily condemned in most of Canada and widely reported by the mainstream media.

In 2009, when retired federal judge Paul Staniszewski, who funded scholarships at the University of Windsor and Osgoode Hall Law School, asked that the scholarships he funded not be given to anyone practicing Islam as a form of "retaliation" to the unrelated decapitation of a Polish engineer beheaded by the Taliban in Pakistan, little was really said or reported. Undoubtedly politics played a part on the very different reactions to these two "racist" events. Despite the fact that what he said may not have been politically correct, what

Premier Parizeau said was truthful. The so-called "ethnic minorities" in Québec did not want to separate and played an important role in voting against Québec's independence or secession. It would be a totally different matter, if Parizeau was implying that his province's ethnic minorities did not have a right to vote or to live in Québec. What is actually more shocking is the mindset and thought process of a federal judge like Staniszewski. What does his attitude say about the latent racism and prejudice in society? What does Staniszewski's attitude say about the potential for animus by individuals in high office and judges who are suppose to secure justice?

Orwellian Semantics: Tolerance as Intolerance

According to Malcolm X, during a 1964 interview with Claude Lewis, an era of hypocrisy had come into place and the "white" dominant group was pretending they wanted the "black" subordinate group to be free and the "blacks" were reciprocally pretending to believe that the "whites" wanted their freedom. While the racial lines that Malcolm draws may be simplistic and not accurate, the point he makes is worth discussing and expanding. This not only relates to what I addressed earlier about the ideas of reform versus revolution, but it also relates to what was said about the inter-racial alliances formed to preserve existing power structures.

It is not out of place at all to ask if members of what can be called "discriminated groups" or minorities in capitalist consumer societies only seek social stratification and upward mobility— comfort and privilege for themselves—rather than equality and justice for their entire group. After all, it can be argued from a conflict perspective that sharing the same societal values and norms as the dominant group, many members of the discriminated groups want the same things and have the same goals.

Functionalists would tend to agree with such an analysis and interactionists would study the effects of dominant normative system on the identities and values of minority members. Furthermore, this is where accusations against U.S. President Barack Hussein Obama as a "race traitor" and "House Negro" come into play. In many cases these "House Negros" as well as the dominant group(s) they represent have actually appropriated anti-racism, twisted it, or used it for careerist goals. This inversely serves racism or at a minimum does not reduce or address it in a society. Gilroy also makes a similar argument in his critique of British anti-racism policies by pointing out that a "black bourgeoisie" has evolved in the United Kingdom that has a strategic interest in maintaining an anti-racism establishment and working in professions like social service work, teaching, and anti-racism policymaking that provide social assistance to "black" Britons.

This hypocrisy is further compounded by the deceptions of a narrative of liberal "tolerance." Ironically, this brand of liberal tolerance does not tolerate any form of dissent. In 1963, Malcolm X touched upon the construction of this illusion during an interview with WUST radio. He would point out that the so-called "white liberals" and supposedly non-racist "white northerners" would be the first to leave urban areas if African-Americans moved in, while the so-called intolerant "white conservatives" would stay longer and live alongside the African-Americans. What we have is a new form of social policing under the pretence and cover of liberal tolerance.

What's more, these policies of tolerance are part of the ideological makeup that serves to support, maintain, and legitimize the plethora of relationships within so-called liberal democracies. This ideological cover serves to enforce hierarchical relations of power and production. Like this book says: "All structures that stabilize and reinforce slave relations while masking or impeding the possibility of rebellion support slavery." Rancourt is absolutely correct and aligned with many other critical thinkers when he says capitalist society "has perfected an illusion of independence."

I would add that in paradox capitalism has also created disarming illusions of "equality" and "collectivity." These illusions are intended to maintain the social order and status quo, while pacifying any resistance to societal integration by various individuals and groups, especially ones being absorbed into the capitalist system like immigrants and conquered peoples being silently colonized by the "market forces" of neo-liberal globalization.

Individuals in so-called industrialized liberal democratic societies and other capitalist societies are structurally forced to be more and more integrated and dependent on the prevailing capitalist economic structure that is controlled in the concentrated hands of a minority. In the first place, interdependence is facilitated in large industrialized societies by a division of labour and the specialization of individuals in their tasks and functions. This leads to what the French scholar Émile Durkheim termed a state of *organic solidarity*. Although not necessarily bad, this interdependence is turned into dependence by those who exploit the relationships of production by controlling the economy or means of production and the socio-political structure of a society. Therefore, this societal state may be referred to as "organic" in Durkheimian analysis, but the "solidarity" is necessitated or coerced on the basis of material needs and is not really a form of solidarity. This structural-functionalist perspective leaves no room for the agency of individuals as societal actors either, but paints an accurate picture of what we can call a de-humanizing and tightening "iron cage" or hardening "shell" that follows the same analytical trajectory as Weber's work on the growing number of limitations being imposed on individual autonomy as a result of the bureaucratization of society.

Opposing the Cultural Mafia In Defence of Racism

It is difficult not to agree with the direction of the analysis regarding institutionalized anti-racism that this book adopts. In my view, its ideas steer readers in the right direction. The position this book takes on institutionalized anti-racism enforces my own positions as a sociologist, which I now summarize.

Denis G. Rancourt

The anti-racism establishment blurs lines and act as a deceptive form of pacifism and cognitive infiltration that is used for conditioning oppressed groups. It is used to prevent subordinated peoples, including the "internally colonized" minorities of a society, from liberating themselves or becoming aware of the true nature of their oppression by de-colonizing their minds. Furthermore, the anti-racism policies of this establishment maintain racism and societal divisions as a means of keeping certain power structures in place. Rancourt says it best when he explains that hierarchy "continuously strives to both disorient and incapacitate the individual in order to maximize its growth in both size and depth."

Borrowing from the Frankfurt School's Theodor Adorno and Max Horkheimer, I have to mention the modern phenomenon of the cultural industry. The manufacturing of taste through this cultural industry is an indispensable part of modern capitalism and its illusions, which subsidizes most groups in society as prisoners of consumerist production. This cultural industry also creates the deadly illusion of free choice for its prisoners. The anti-racism establishment (or at least a segment of it) is akin to the Frankfurt School's concept of the cultural industry, because it also creates an illusion and works to transform the enforcement and appearance of power differentials. This modern anti-racism establishment creates the mirage of tolerance where there is really intolerance and at the same time serves to maintain the structure of power by projecting the image of group equality where there is really inequality. At the same time its enforcers are predominately the "Uncle Toms" and "House Negros" or new ethnic minority bourgeoisie that Gilroy criticises.

This anti-racism establishment can be extremely intolerant of any alternative narratives or views as a means of maintaining its mirage. Dissidents are censored and persecuted under the protective cover of the language of tolerance and of fighting bigotry. This includes language policing, which is one of the most effective tools for defining concepts. Language is not only important for the production of meaning, but it is also undividable from the production of power. Why else would the Turkish government have outlawed the Kurdish language from being spoken by the large population of Kurds inside Turkey?

Inside Canada, not only has there been variant forms of language policing against English conducted on behalf of the Francophone majority in Québec, but the reverse has also been true in the case of Anglophone repression of French inside and outside of the province of Québec.

Furthermore, those with an eye for gender analysis would quickly draw our attention to the different common titles used for men (Mr.) in the English language versus those addressing women (Miss, Mrs., and Ms.) in English. Such a use of language is tied to gender scripts and reveals the marital status of women unlike those of men. It was also formerly considered incorrect to mention or write the word woman before the word man; the order of ranking had to always be the word man followed by the word woman. Not only are roles being prescribed and proscribed through language, but power relationships and social concepts are also being projected through it. This is why the anti-racism establishment and what I call the "cultural mafia," which includes the intelligentsia and mass media, that serves power police language and expression. It is a term that is akin to Rancourt's "service intellectuals" and the petty-bourgeois intellectual class that the Marxists have long described.

Language policing is just one component for the safeguarding of modern power structures. The cultural mafia's work does much more than police culture and expression. Alongside the anti-racism establishment the cultural mafia try to police and authorize all other counter-discourses and forms of dissent.

Affirmative action, activism, and the definitions of what is correct and what is not are all managed by this cultural mafia that has tried to monopolize and define the boundaries of gender analysis, culture critique, and sociological discourses. Repeating myself, I have to emphasize that these forces work to regulate criticism and to authorize what forms of criticism are "valid." Thus this cultural mafia maintains the status quo of societal relationships and power in a suffocating climate of progressive service for the so-called "betterment of society."

A Return to Radical Perspectives

Deception is a key feature of capitalism and capitalist societies, especially under neo-liberalism. Sophistry and a "sea of deception" are involved in maintaining power relationships. The welfare state is a means to pacify workers from revolting against the ruling class. Some of the basic needs of the lower classes are provided by the ruling class. The working class recipients of this public welfare, such as healthcare, ironically are the producers of the capital behind the welfare they themselves receive, but are told to be thankful to the ruling class, which is actually siphoning most the capital for itself. Under the banner of fairness, laws reinforce societal hierarchies and inequality. Individuals are increasingly making more and more constrained or coerced choices with little alternatives whereas a mirage of freedom of unrestrained choice is an integral part of daily life.

So-called humanitarian interventions in foreign countries are self-serving military endeavours for the foreign interventionists who profit from them and maintain de facto colonial international relationships. Foreign development work is used to enforce dependency and maintain old colonial relationships. Large segments of indigenous peoples throughout the world are kept as prisoners of a binary concept of a dynamic state of modernity and a static state of pre-industrial primitive indigeneity.

This binary script seeks to conscript indigenous people as what the Columbian anthropologist Astrid Ulloa calls mythical *ecological natives* that are not allowed to adapt to modern technology or to change as a means of utilizing their land rights and natural resources for economic gains. Indigenous peoples that change are viewed as losing their identities and simultaneously their claims to their lands;

their claims to their land can only be justified under this binary layout if they are ecological natives living in a static state as "noble savages." Capitalism seeks to appropriate their lands and rights through this binary layout.

Critical race theory emphasises that racism and inequality are most efficiently documented by listening to people about their experiences and views about race. This is something that the politically correct anti-racism regimes of different states have actually hurt through censorship.

Critical race theory only receives lip service now. While the anti-racism establishment preaches equality and tolerance, ironically it is intolerant to diversity of thought and free speech.

Gilroy has condemned anti-racism in its institutional form and argued that on the basis of misconstrued standpoints on race that anti-racism has been taken in the wrong direction. He convincingly argued for an authentic radical critique of the "moralistic excesses" practiced in the name of anti-racism in the United Kingdom. For Gilroy, class analysis sits at the heart of racism and he has criticized the ridiculous and absurd things that have been done in the name of anti-racism and anti-racist orthodoxy, which he has argued have actually been harmful towards fighting biases, prejudice, xenophobia, and bigotry. For him the real goal has been "black emancipation" and not the simplistic critiques of racism by the British anti-racism movement that has failed to recognize the roots of racism and its functions. Gilroy maintained that anti-racism has defanged the fight against oppression by pacifying oppressed groups by suggesting that racism can be eliminated on its own if it was merely repressed.

The anti-racism establishment has merely trivialized the struggle against racism and actually served to isolate it from the real political struggles between the dominant and subordinate classes. The message is clear: people should not be united by the colour of their skin or ethnicity, but by their politics and struggles. Moreover, Gilroy has argued that "black" Britons needed to let go of the concepts of "victimhood" and that a false consciousness about race also brought politically opposed groups together on the basis of racial identity instead of on the basis of political struggle and historic experiences of repression.

There is also a link between ideas of race and ethnicity with concepts of nationhood and nationalism. The jump from racism to nationalism is not too great as Adolph Hitler's German National Socialism or Nazism in the Third Reich illustrates. Gilroy's position about a false racial consciousness among "black" Britons is similar to the earlier position that Marxist intellectual and anti-war activist Rosa Luxemburg took against nationalism. Luxemburg maintained that nationalism and regionalism were forces that disarmed subordinated groups while maintaining the power of the capitalist elites over them. She argued that nationalism was used to create a false consciousness that prevented subordinated groups, specifically the proletariat, from revolting against the status quo. An ethnic Pole herself that was born in what was at the time the Russian Empire, Luxemburg was opposed to the Polish nationalist (and essentially ethnic-based) discourse in Vistula Land (Russian Poland). She argued that the "right of self-determination" was misunderstood and corrupted; the nationalist discourse in Vistula Land merely served to distract and misguide the majority of Poles from reaching their goals of true emancipation by diluting their efforts for genuine self-determination through the illusion that nationalist secession would solve all their problems.

While Rancourt argues on one track for racialization as a means of reorganization and emancipation, ultimately and in paradox his writing works for a de-racialized world. The oppressed must save themselves and the oppressors, and not vice-versa. His work is a return to the liberation ideology that filled the world during de-colonization after the Second World War.

This book also criticizes anti-racism by arguing that suppressing racism is not enough or right, because it is really a force of avoidance. Taboos preventing discussion on the subject only act like a wall or barrier. Problems that have been swept under the rug really need to be brought to a table and solved. This is the most democratic thing to

33

do. Talking about racist feelings, through what is called *communicative action* in the public arena is much more efficient than forcing people to hide their racisms. If "the emperor has no clothes," we should all be able to say it.

Rancourt puts it best: "Free expression between individuals is the basis of coexistence, cooperation, and politics." He insists that free expression really means free expression and not some other Orwellian meaning. As a gadfly, he resists all normative guidelines that would channel our "free expression" into being what the cultural mafia would call "constructive" or "rational" or "respectful" and so on. This all flies in the face of the political correctness which, Denis Rancourt argues, is to be rejected as a force suffocating the much needed openness all societies need.

—Mahdi Darius Nazemroaya

Mahdi Darius Nazemroaya is a sociologist, award-winning author, and noted geopolitical analyst. His articles on topics such as international relations and the global system have been translated into more than twenty-five languages around the world, including German, Italian, Arabic, Chinese, Spanish, Russian, Turkish, Japanese, and Portuguese. The Globalization of NATO, with its foreword written by former United Nations assistant secretary-general Denis J. Halliday, is one of his latest published works. In 2011, he was a correspondent for the investigative news program Flashpoints, which is broadcast by more than fifty stations in North America and produced from Berkley, California. In the same year he received special mention from the Latin American Federation of Journalists (FELAP) as a correspondent in North Africa and was also awarded the prestigious First National Prize of the Mexican Press Club for his work in the field of international journalism. He is a member of the Scientific Committee of Geopolitica, a peer-reviewed journal of geopolitics in Italy, and in affiliation with the European Centre for the Study of Interventionism has worked on the production of documentaries about world issues. He currently works at Carleton University, where his teaching duties have included Latin American studies, African history, and introductory sociology.

Denis G. Rancourt

Author's Introduction and Overview

I HAVE PERSONAL experience with "racial" oppression in that I grew up as a French Canadian in a staunchly anti-French community, North Bay, Ontario, in the 1960s. The antagonism was crass and cruel. The oppression was physical and palpable. I was regularly spat on, intimidated, and physically beat up for being a "frog" or for uttering French words. There were no French free zones in public places, except Catholic French schools and churches which my family attended. The walk between school and home was a dangerous route that I feared, day after day, year after year.

I learned English very quickly. The first English word I learned at the age of five in my new English neighbourhood was "shut up". My mother was distressed to explain what it meant. I did everything I could to become English. I was "self" motivated to switch to English education as soon as I could in university. I did everything I could to integrate. Only later did I realize what I had lost and did I start to recover, at first thanks to the pleasure of teaching in French at the University of Ottawa, in Canada's "bilingual" capital city.

I have actually suffered more, in my life as a whole, from insidious class oppression than from the Ontario French-English divide. However, recently, I was accused of malice for exercising my nominal right and requesting to be heard in French in the *Ontario Superior Court of Justice*, where the Anglophone master (judge) suggested that punitive "Costs Thrown Away" would be an appropriate remedy awarded to the other party to the litigation.[1]

Neither of my parents went to university. My mother did not finish high school and my father did not finish primary school and could not easily read or write. I was not headed for the middle class. I did not aspire to the middle class. A classmate in primary school once blurted out about me, in English, in an in-class "what are you going to be" session: "Smartest kid in the class and he wants to be a grease monkey." I took the mechanical option in high school, and I loved it. Later, following a shift caused by a family rupture and then years of study at several universities, I would write scientific papers about quantum mechanics and teach quantum mechanics at the university level, but not before being thoroughly "class handled".

For decades, I was forced to study and work in an environment where the working class was continually and actively denigrated, until I started inviting the working class, and all societal classes, into my university courses.[2] The latter project, initiated in 2005, caused me to be disciplined, but a binding labour arbitration award found that all my pedagogical methods were within the purview of my academic freedom[3]. Nonetheless, I was fired in 2009 from my

---

[1] Court transcript of January 26, 2012 case management hearing before Master MacLeod:
http://rancourt.academicfreedom.ca/Data/uofowatch/2012-01-26=Case-Conference-w-Master-MacLead.PDF

[2] Rancourt, Denis, *Academic Squatting: A democratic method of curriculum development*, Our Schools Our Selves, V. 16 N. 3 (#87) Spring 2007, p. 105-109.

[3] *Association of Professors of the University of Ottawa v. University of Ottawa*, Grievance Arbitration, [2008] O.L.A.A. No. 356 (QL), Arbitrator Michel G. Picher, Grievor Denis G. Rancourt, released June 25, 2008. http://lancasterhouse.com/pdf/decisions/up-PicherM_UniversityofOttawa.pdf
Teaching Science through Social Activism is Protected by Academic Freedom, Arbitrator Rules, *College and University Employment Law E-Bulletin*, February

tenured full professorship for my free expression in many spheres, under the false pretext of fraudulent grading in a one-semester advanced physics course. My firing is a major academic freedom case in Canada and will continue to be before a labour tribunal until at least 2013.[4]

I have no self-illusion that this book will enlighten or cause any change. I don't believe a book can do that. I believe the proverbial phrase that "the pen is mightier than the sword" is the opposite of what should be obvious to anyone: physical force and the threat of physical force are unquestionably the drivers in the relations of domination that characterize human societies. It is remarkable that any student of history could repeat such nonsense as represented by that vacuous and shallow phrase.

The indoctrination towards ascribing relevance to the written word as a vector of "powerful ideas" is so strong among service intellectuals in our managed societies, however, that I have no doubt that many readers will mine these pages for the "useful ideas" that they may contain, or for any contribution to the "discourse of ideas" – which is wrongly considered to be the lifeblood of a healthy modern society.

Wrong, of course, because this allowed-discourse of intellectuals must be a discourse outside of praxis[5] or risk. It must be cerebral because the more cerebral it is, the deeper it is and therefore

---

17, 2009, Issue No. 23.
http://rancourt.academicfreedom.ca/Data/Documents/law-e-bulletin-analysis-picher-arbitration.pdf

[4] Rancourt, Denis, June 2011 statement, *This is what targeting a dissident tenured professor looks like in Canada*,
http://rancourt.academicfreedom.ca/background/targetingadissident.html

[5] I use the term "praxis" to mean an inseparable and synergetic fusion of action and reflection as part of one's struggle for liberation, as defined by Paulo Freire.

the greater its impact on the real world, somehow. This is the Möbius strip of the service intellectual. And the service intellectual must construct and maintain such self-image buffers on the scale of the entire functioning society, lest we become conscious of the extreme violence to which we are subjected and to which we collectively subject others.

For the most part, I write as part of my praxis of liberation, fighting my own oppression, in the sense explained by Paulo Freire in his seminal work.[6] Therefore, I pessimistically expect that only those involved in their own Freirian praxes, fighting their own oppressions rather than some displaced injustice, might derive useful benefit from these notes. I combine this pessimism of the mind with optimism of the will[7], which motivates me to write.

This book is also outreach for fighters in the trenches and it is a way for me to test my ideas. And it is a contradiction. I was groomed as a service intellectual. My hierarchical purpose was that of service intellectual. I too long for the pure rationality of expressed ideas to somehow be of use, against all odds. In this sense, therefore, this book is more than reflections and analysis accompanying a praxis, it is also a desperate and irrational act—such an act that is typical of the true intellectual, in the sense explained by Edward Said.[8]

Otherwise, how does one rebel against the machine while maintaining enough ties to it to not be crushed by the gears? How does one send out smoke signals without being annihilated by the cavalry? How does one use camouflage without integration into the environment?

An honest book from praxis is a dangerous thing. Did Che

---

[6] Freire, Paulo, *Pedagogy of the Oppressed*, 1970; Continuum, NY, 2000.

[7] "I'm a pessimist because of intelligence, but an optimist because of will." Antonio Gramsci, Letter from Prison (19 December 1929). Source: Wikiquote.

[8] Said, Edward, *Representations of the Intellectual*, 1994; Vintage Books, NY, 1996.

Guevara imagine that his *Guerrilla Warfare*[9] would become a training manual for the CIA in exterminating armed resistance by genocidal cleansing? Likewise, on a more superficial plane, will my ideas be turned against free speech advocates by guiding a perfected sophistry of the benefits of state control and surveillance? This is an unavoidable risk in attempting to project one's influence with written words. It is one of the intrinsic risks of communication.

Outside of hierarchy's grip and its internal air-tight logic of self-definition, have my reflections produced anything that can guide a continued praxis of liberation? I think so. Here is one example. Possibly the newest or most counter-current idea in these pages is the idea that racism in itself is neither good nor bad, any more than hate, as a human emotion, is, in itself, neither good nor bad.

Both racism and hate, in their unadulterated forms, are spontaneous human animal reactions to aggression and oppression. As such, they are natural reactions which have survived evolution ever since animals have had emotions[10], and which continue to serve vital roles in species survival and in individual preservation.

By "unadulterated form", I mean not manipulated by social engineering or hierarchical machination. For example, the sentiment of love can be highly adulterated and manipulated in a hierarchical context. We should not respond by banning love to prevent its denaturalization. Nevertheless, banning (constraining, certifying, delimiting) love is most common in organized religion and in society at large. In this way, natural impulses and primordial emotions can all be twisted and entangled to maintain an array of individual identities defined by and dependent on the hierarchy. Guilt, normalcy, acceptance, and status are used to confine and direct impulses and emotions in such a way as to lock the individual into his/her place.

The natural animal impulses and emotional reactions have

---

[9] Guevara, Che, *Guerrilla Warfare*, 1961.

[10] Darwin, Charles, *The Expression of the Emotions in Man and Animals*, 1872.

developed and adapted during one hundred million years of small-scale mammalian communities, and are thereby not suited to modern human hierarchies supported by advanced technology which have emerged in the last millisecond in the hour of life on the planet. Therefore, a main concern in highly stratified human dominance hierarchies is managing or manipulating (mostly suppressing) natural emotional reactions.

World travellers will have noted the striking brilliance of authentic emotions in societies which are less hierarchical, where communities are less confined by top-down rules in every detail of thought and expression. The same observation can be made in comparing a family with an authoritarian patriarch to one where "kids will be kids". Highly hierarchical systems are destabilized by freedom. In such systems freedom must be managed and true freedom must be replaced with canned substitutes. If pockets or areas of freedom are allowed or are defended, then hierarchical sharpening, the spontaneous increase of hierarchical structure and control, is frustrated.

A main device in the suppression of free emotional expression, which serves hierarchical maintenance, is the ludicrous and widespread dogma of "bad" and "good" emotions, which is accompanied by such trappings as the virtue of "moderation" and the vice of "excess". If a social feedback can be established which blunts, attenuates, moderates, criminalizes, etc., emotions and reactions, then we are on the road to a stable highly stratified hierarchy (of sick and atrophied individuals).

If we reject the hierarchy's suppression of our emotional reactions, then we regain the capacity to self-organize and self-govern our local environments. We recover our persons and our individual capacities to be political, influential, engaged…we start to make our own neighbourhoods, our own work environments, and so on. We become cooperative between ourselves and unmanageable from the top.

For such active liberation to flourish and continuously renew itself, "emotional conflict" must be alive and well, rather than suppressed from above. You learn to handle "emotional conflict" and you grow in "emotional conflict" via its practice, by speaking your mind, by testing your influence, by making up, and so on. Racism, hate, anger, love and compassion in individuals is all part of the mix. It's all humans reacting and interacting.

Whereas individuals must organize to fight against the hate and racism of the oppressive hierarchy, to fight their common oppressions, we must not conflate our own anger and hate, which are reactions of self-defence, with any feature of the oppressor. One hate is based in preservation while the other is based in dominance. One is personal, authentic, and dissipates when the threat is momentarily removed or when another emotion replaces it while the other is systematic, voracious, and does not dissipate.

If we accept one thesis of this book, that racism is metabolic and has an evolutionary root, and if we trust that interacting humans not overly oppressed by superior hierarchical forces will work things out, then we must recognize that outlawing racist opinion and racist reactions is part of a hierarchical oppression, an attack against natural metabolic reactions, an attack which supports hierarchical domination, and that such suppression of individual expression can only make matters worse and deepen denial.

This is not a superficial justification for allowing racial mobbing in our local environments. It is a model that racial mobbing is best addressed at its local root, and continuously addressed as part of the community's self-definition. It is a model that superstructure policing of attitudes, thoughts, and words can only maintain hierarchical oppression and prevent self-determination.

To argue for judicial and administrative controls on language, attitudes, and beliefs, however disagreeable we imagine these might be, is to infantilize and incapacitate the individual in his/her community. It is to enable the hand of hierarchical power to regulate and prevent human development and liberation. It is to prevent the individual both from knowing himself/herself and from knowing his/her neighbour.

For me to have to actually explain this is a sign of our times. For me to have to make this argument is in itself frightening. For me to have to explain that it's best to keep Big Brother out of this one is surrealistic. I believe Canadian society has significantly evolved towards Fascism since I was a young child in the 1960s.[11] I believe this Fascism can be clearly traced in the evolution of "our" institutions. But I also have seen it in the eyes of the young university students that I followed for more than thirty years and as an undergraduate myself at first. I think the individual is dramatically determined by the institutional environment and the degree of Fascism in a society can be directly gauged by the degree to which individuals feel and visualize themselves as powerful. Not empowered to succeed by integration, but personally powerful and radically communicative.

Does the Right bring on Fascism or is the Right a response to Fascism? I'm thinking now the latter. The institutions and Fascism have evolved under the Left in Canada, under the Liberals. People needing to break out are drawn to a Right that purports to dismantling big government and that appeals to individual and small-scale autonomy. The rise of the Right may well be a swing back against decades of creeping Fascism. But the actual hierarchical bosses are still in charge so there will need to be a true emergence of conflict. I don't think that there are enough pharmaceuticals and iPhone apps manufactured to keep a lid on it much longer. We are going to have to be real, soon, because they want everything.

Race will be part of it, as will gender, but the real battle is for freedom. Those in the ghettos defined by the bosses will be working for the bosses.

---

[11] Rancourt, D.G., *Canadian Education as an Impetus towards Fascism*, 2009 vol.1 issue.2 of JASTE (*Journal for Activist Science & Technology Education*), pages 68-77. http://www.wepaste.org/Resources/JASTE1-2f_Rancourt.pdf

Free expression between individuals is the basis of coexistence, cooperation, and politics. In peace time, authentic speech exchanged with one's opponents is the only road towards real solutions anchored in a stable justice. This is true in a society like ours, which is not in the midst of a civil war, where it is possible to face one's antagonists in several informal and institutional venues and using an array of communications media. If it's worth talking to resolve differences then it's worth talking frankly, without censorship or self-censorship.

In the words of Malcolm X:[12]

> *The only way the problem can be solved—first, the white man and the black man have to be able to sit down at the same table. The white man has to feel free to speak his mind without hurting the feelings of that Negro, and the so-called Negro has to feel free to speak his mind without hurting the feelings of the white man. Then they can bring the issues that are under the rug out on top of the table and take an intelligent approach to get the problem solved.*

To "sit at the same table" one party needs to fight its way out from under the table and force the other party to sit rather than tower over the table. The dominant party will not spontaneously give up its dominance. Only the oppressed can liberate themselves, thereby humanizing the oppressor. This principle of liberation was spelled out by Freire. There are no known exceptions in history. Power accommodates itself when it is forced to do so, within a logic of pain versus gain in minimizing any loss of control.

In this liberation struggle, free expression, if it were to exist, would be entirely to the advantage of the oppressed and entirely to

---

[12] *My Philosophy is Black Nationalism* speech, Youtube: http://youtu.be/Ix2-m1gDX8s

the disadvantage of the oppressor—a truth the oppressor will do everything to mask (including manufacture an industry of "transparency" managed by faithful service intellectuals, and so on). This truth about free expression does not arise from "the power of words" but rather from the power of individual praxis to collectivize struggles.

The "critical race theory" first advanced by academic designers (critics, lobbyists, cheerleaders) of the legal apparatus[13] is one of many devices to constrain free expression to the benefit of society's dominance hierarchy, whether or not this was the conscious intention. Such constraints, once internalized, prevent individual emancipation by preventing authentic interactions and, therefore, quell free expression in its home, the individual. Its most prominent academic critic has been Henry Louis Gates Jr.[14]

Another point that I advance in this book and which is usually not represented (or underrepresented) in studies of racism is the following: any study of hierarchical oppression, whether the oppression is primarily based on race or class or another defining characteristic, must include the dimension of control over expression, and, therefore, in turn, must include a prominent consideration of the systemic role of elite collaborators drawn from the oppressed group.

Rewarded collaboration by chosen individuals from the oppressed group is not an incidental phenomenon. It is the crux of a stable and working system of hierarchical dominance. All the bosses understand this. This is the role of a "bosses union" in a labour

---

[13] Matsuda, Mari, Lawrence, Charles R. III, and Delgado, Richard, *Words that Wound: Critical Race Theory, Assaultive Speech, and the First Amendment*, Westview Press, Boulder, Colo., 1993.

[14] Gates, Henry Jouis Jr., *Critical Race Theory and Freedom of Speech*, Chapter Five in "The Future of Academic Freedom", Menard, Louis, Ed., University of Chicago Press, 1996.

context where union executives have class association with the managers. This is why there are middle managers, and a whole hierarchical chain of command: Each command layer is closest in character to the group it directly commands. A system in which the overtly oppressed class is completely separated from the oppressor is an unstable system that will spontaneously generate revolt. Even a prison environment needs collaboration for stabilization. Iron bars and the threat of brute force are insufficient. Force is sufficient only when its purpose is to exterminate.

If the goal is to oppress and exploit rather than simply exterminate, then owned-collaborators are essential. And the role of the collaborator is actuated via expression. The collaborator is a "good cop" and the "bad cop" is never far away. The good cop "reasons" and lays out a mental environment of the benefits of voluntary compliance. In a hierarchy of dominance with an identifiable oppressed group, the establishment and its police and harsh rules are the bad cop, whereas the hired collaborator is the good cop mediator and attitude doctor.

There is a full array of collaborators matched to the complexity of the hierarchy. These are: the bosses unions, the non-government organizations (NGOs), the service intellectuals, the public relations experts, the counsellors, the health professionals, and so on.

In the context of racial oppression, the elite collaborators have been termed "house negroes," or Uncle Toms. Malcolm X spelled out their use by the white establishment in the context of Black revolutionary movements of the 1950s and 1960s in his *Message to the Grassroots* speech, in part[15]:

> *[...]*
> *Just as the slavemaster of that day used Tom, the*

---

[15] Malcolm X, *Message to the Grassroots*, speech, November 10, 1963, Detroit, Michigan.
http://www.sojust.net/speeches/malcolm_x_message.html

house Negro, to keep the field Negroes in check, the same old slavemaster today has Negroes who are nothing but modern Uncle Toms, 20th century Uncle Toms, to keep you and me in check, keep us under control, keep us passive and peaceful and nonviolent. That's Tom making you nonviolent. It's like when you go to the dentist, and the man's going to take your tooth. You're going to fight him when he starts pulling. So he squirts some stuff in your jaw called novocaine, to make you think they're not doing anything to you. So you sit there and 'cause you've got all of that novocaine in your jaw, you suffer peacefully. Blood running all down your jaw, and you don't know what's happening. 'Cause someone has taught you to suffer—peacefully.

The white man do the same thing to you in the street, when he want to put knots on your head and take advantage of you and don't have to be afraid of your fighting back. To keep you from fighting back, he gets these old religious Uncle Toms to teach you and me, just like novocaine, suffer peacefully. Don't stop suffering—just suffer peacefully. As Reverend Cleage pointed out, "Let your blood flow In the streets." This is a shame. And you know he's a Christian preacher. If it's a shame to him, you know what it is to me.

There's nothing in our book, the Quran—you call it "Ko-ran"—that teaches us to suffer peacefully. Our religion teaches us to be intelligent. Be peaceful, be courteous, obey the law, respect everyone; but if someone puts his hand on you, send him to the cemetery. That's a good religion. In fact, that's that old-time religion. That's the one that Ma and Pa used to talk about: an eye for an eye, and a tooth for a tooth, and a head for a head, and a life for a life: That's a good religion. And doesn't nobody resent that kind of religion being taught but a wolf, who intends to make you his meal.

This is the way it is with the white man in America. He's a wolf and you're sheep. Any time a shepherd, a pastor, teach you and me not to run from the white man and, at the same time, teach us not to fight the white man, he's a traitor to you and me. Don't lay down our life all by itself. No, preserve your life. It's the best thing you got. And if you got to give it up, let it be even-steven.

The slavemaster took Tom and dressed him well, and fed him well, and even gave him a little education—a little education; gave him a long coat and a top hat and made all the other slaves look up to him. Then he used Tom to control them. The same strategy that was used in those days is used today, by the same white man. He takes a Negro, a so-called Negro, and make him prominent, build him up, publicize him, make him a celebrity. And then he becomes a spokesman for Negroes—and a Negro leader.

I would like to just mention just one other thing else quickly, and that is the method that the white man uses, how the white man uses these "big guns," or Negro leaders, against the black revolution. They are not a part of the Negro revolution. They are used against the Negro revolution.

[…]

It was the grass roots out there in the street. [It] scared the white man to death, scared the white power structure in Washington, D. C. to death; I was there. When they found out that this black

> *steamroller was going to come down on the capital,*
> *they called in Wilkins; they called in Randolph; they*
> *called in these national Negro leaders that you*
> *respect and told them, "Call it off." Kennedy said,*
> *"Look, you all letting this thing go too far." And Old*
> *Tom said, "Boss, I can't stop it, because I didn't start*
> *it." I'm telling you what they said. They said, "I'm*
> *not even in it, much less at the head of it." They said,*
> *"These Negroes are doing things on their own.*
> *They're running ahead of us." And that old shrewd*
> *fox, he said, "Well If you all aren't in it, I'll put you*
> *in it. I'll put you at the head of it. I'll endorse it. I'll*
> *welcome it. I'll help it. I'll join it."*
>
> *[...]*

Put succinctly, at an individual level and in terms of expression, Malcolm X explained it as[16]:

> *Back during slavery, when Black people like me*
> *talked to the slaves, they didn't kill 'em, they sent*
> *some old house Negro along behind him to undo what*
> *he said. You have to read the history of slavery to*
> *understand this. There were two kinds of Negroes.*
> *There was that old house Negro and the field Negro.*

Malcolm X exposed collaborators at a time when false and stratified integration was being developed and institutionalized as an effective pacifier. In all revolutions, a major task is the identification and removal of collaborators, because in all dominance hierarchies, collaborators are essential as the main counter revolutionary tool.

A corollary to the latter rule is that, in a stable dominance

---

[16] *Malcolm X: The House Negro and the Field Negro*, YouTube video of a 1963(?) speech, http://youtu.be/znQe9nUKzvQ

hierarchy, exposing collaborators carries a high price. The backlash to even a black person who calls out a "house negro" is significant.

In the interest of frankness, I must express my own run-in with a backlash from using the term "house negro". In my case the backlash takes the form of an on-going $1 million defamation lawsuit against me that was initiated in 2011[17] after I had been removed from my tenured full professorship in 2009.

It is an aggressive civil lawsuit using one of Canada's largest law firms and one of Canada's leading defamation lawyers, where, as an unemployed defendant, I am self-represented. The plaintiff is a black law professor at my former university, the University of Ottawa, and her private litigation is entirely funded by the university, without a spending limit.[18]

At stake are my freedom of expression, my life savings (which will be exhausted at the time of printing), my future pension payments, and potentially my family's home. The plaintiff did not claim any demonstrable damage, nor does the law require her to prove any damage.[19] A lawsuit such as this has several "mini trials" which are called "motions" and which determine procedural points such as the scope of the evidence or which attempt to re-define or stay the action. Even though I do not pay a lawyer for my defence, each time I lose a motion, the Court orders me to pay the legal fees of the other side. Over twenty motions have been initiated to date. Each one is a demanding process with specialized documents, rules of evidence, cross-examinations, court hearings, and so on.

In 2008, the student union released a public report about

---

[17] Links to all court documents and transcripts:
http://rancourt.academicfreedom.ca/background/stlewislawsuit.html
[18] "Without a cap", in the words of university president Allan Rock, in sworn testimony under cross-examination, April 18, 2012.
[19] *Libel and Slander Act*, R.S.O. 1990, CHAPTER L.12.
http://www.e-
laws.gov.on.ca/html/statutes/english/elaws_statutes_90l12_e.htm

systemic racism at the University of Ottawa.[20] The University responded by asking the said law professor expert to assess the student report in a responding public report. The expert found that there was no firm basis for affirming systemic racism at the University of Ottawa. In the expert author's words, in part[21]:

> *The short answer for this evaluator on whether there is systemic racism in the administration of the Academic Fraud process at the University of Ottawa is: I don't know. What I do know, is that this report does not establish this in any measurable or analytically plausible fashion.*

I run a blog critical of the University of Ottawa and I was critical of the expert's report in a 2008 blogpost.[22] Some three years later, after the student union released relevant access to information documents in 2011, I blogged again stating that the access to information documents suggested that the expert had acted as the house negro of the university president. The 2011 blogpost was entitled *Did Professor Joanne St. Lewis act as Allan Rock's house negro?* and my exact words were[23]:

---

[20] *Mistreatment of Students, Unfair Practices and Systemic Racism at the University of Ottawa*, Annual Report, November 2008, Student Appeal Centre (SAC), Student Federation University of Ottawa (SFUO).

[21] *Evaluation Report of Student Appeal Centre 2008 Annual Report*, November 15, 2008, Professor Joanne St. Lewis.
http://web5.uottawa.ca/admingov/documents/evaluation-report-sac-2008-annual-report.pdf

[22] *Rock Administration Prefers to Confuse 'Independent' with 'Internal' Rather Than Address Systemic Racism*, December 6, 2008, Denis G. Rancourt.
http://uofowatch.blogspot.ca/2008/12/rock-administration-prefers-to-confuse.html

[23] *Did Professor Joanne St. Lewis act as Allan Rock's house negro?*, February 11, 2011, Denis G. Rancourt.

> *The Student Appeal Centre (SAC) of the student*
> *union at the University of Ottawa today released*
> *documents obtained by an access to information (ATI)*
> *request that suggest that law professor Joanne St.*
> *Lewis acted like president Allan Rock's house negro*
> *when she enthusiastically toiled to discredit a 2008*
> *SAC report about systemic racial discrimination at*
> *the university.*

In the same blogpost, I also explained and defined the political racial term "house negro" by embedding a YouTube video of a classic speech by Malcolm X (see blogpost).

In a recent development, I asked a judge in court to adjourn the day's session so that I could bring a motion to request his recusal on the grounds of reasonable apprehension of bias. The judge had not disclosed that he had funded an endowment fund at the University of Ottawa or that his son had been a lawyer in the national law firm acting for the University in the case (in certain motions the University has party status) and that the law firm had named a meeting room in honour of his son.

The judge reacted by threatening me with contempt of court (a criminal offence) if I persisted in advancing my request, and, after taking a break, recused himself for the reason given that my behaviour had so "disgusted" him that he could not be fair in my regard. This was reported in the Canadian media.[24]

A main argument of the plaintiff in the case is that my fair comment defence for matters of public interest is invalidated by

---

http://uofowatch.blogspot.ca/2011/02/did-professor-joanne-st-lewis-act-as.html

[24] *'Ambush' caused judge to withdraw from 'House Negro' civil suit, lawyers say*, July 27, 2012, Neco Cockburn, *Ottawa Citizen*.

malice because, it is alleged, my language was racist. The plaintiff's main legal argument is that I am racist in saying what I said, and therefore have no defence. In legal defamation, guilt is automatic if one has no valid defence.

The degree to which I am a racist can be judged by all those who wish to do so. One thing is clear: I have direct and extensive experience with the legal apparatus of control of expression in a context of racial oppression. This is the same legal apparatus, in all its majesty[25], that the original critical race theory authors would have us trust, once suitably modified, to regulate racial language and attitudes.

In this and other regards, I feel particularly qualified to write this book. In addition, my independence of thought from any institution, government, employer, or corporation cannot reasonably be challenged.

Most of this book is a selection of my essays originally published on my *Activist Teacher* blog and in various other venues, with new essays and an author's forward added to make a whole. Some of the essays have been translated into several languages and re-posted all over the web.

I have woven the selected essays together and added chapters to make what I hope is a coherent and self-contained main point about racism: that racism cannot be justly and beneficially managed from above, that the only true basis for fighting racism is authentic liberation praxis of individuals. And, that race management from above and using the establishment's elite collaborators must be rejected because it necessarily has a deleterious impact on the true liberation struggle against racism. Collaboration is not liberation.

---

[25] *The law, in its majestic equality, forbids the rich and the poor alike to sleep under bridges, to beg in the streets, and to steal bread.* In: *Le Lys rouge*, Anatole France, 1894.

Denis G. Rancourt

In the words of Mary Mother Jones:[26]

> *I want you to know that this man Jones who is running for mayor of your beautiful city is no relative of mine; no, sir. He belongs to that school of reformers who say capital and labour must join hands. He may be alright. He prays a good deal. But, I wonder if you would shake hands with me if I robbed you. He builds parks to make his workmen contented. But a contented workman is no good. All progress stops in the contented man. I'm for agitation. It's the greater factor for progress.*

I would add that in the "contented man" progress is actively reverted by the advancing dominance hierarchy, as "his" consciousness, dignity, and independence are buried ever more deeply.

I dedicate this collection to my late friend and renowned historian of technology David F. Noble. David taught us by words and by praxis that we learn about the system that controls our lives by opposing it. David's greatest pedagogical tool was personal resistance. By applying David's method of being independent and of getting off one's knees, I have learned more about the world and about myself than I ever would have. I would have died a much more shallow and wretched human being had I not followed my path inspired by Noble, Freire, Malatesta, Bakunin, Mother Jones, Malcolm X, and many others.

Racism is a "popular topic" for intellectuals because most peoples on Earth have suffered from racism enacted against them. Racism is a "popular topic" because many individuals in multi-cultural modern societies have deeply suffered from racism. Racism is a

---

[26] Mother Mary Jones, Speech in Memorial Hall, Toledo, March 24, 1903. In: *Mother Jones Speaks*, Edited by Philip S. Foner, Monad Press, NY, 1983, p.98.

"popular topic" because it can and is used and manipulated by society's managers. But racism is not a "topic". It is not an isolated concept or a societal characteristic that can be evaluated on a yardstick.

The managers would have us believe that "racism", "crime", "poverty", "education", "democracy", and so on, are societal characteristics that can be parameterized as scalars from zero to one hundred percent; that not enough or too much is bad, and that more or less is better. In this way, the system removes meaning from these words by distancing them from their defining contexts of dominance exploitation to leave us only bookkeeping measures of power's success at managing us, to leave us only hockey scores and interest rates on mortgages.

In this book, I make a conscious effort to not treat racism as a topic but instead to root the discussion in a major consideration of the biological, metabolic, psychological, ecological, and evolutionary foundations of racism. If we imagine racism to be a simple feature of society that can be eliminated, as we would eliminate "crime", rather than consider it to be an intrinsic feature of human interactions, which is predominantly influenced by society's dominance hierarchy and class politics of oppression, then we will be working in a parallel universe of policy development which only amplifies the pathological separation between self and community imposed by the dominance hierarchy.

I have come to believe that recent "anti-racism", ushered in with the new legal philosophy known as "critical race theory", and representing policy, law, and educational programs geared towards preventing racism by censoring racist speech, is—to put it kindly—an endeavour pointed in a wrong direction.

It was not difficult for me to come to the latter starting point. The first time I heard about the benefit of white guilt for improving the world I felt nauseous. Yes, I have survivor guilt[27], but guilt is

---

[27] Middle-class whites can have a variety of survivor guilt, normally

paralyzing whereas liberation stems from confidence. Yes, it's difficult to be disadvantaged and to not be part of the dominant group, but liberation has never come from asking the dominant group to be more accommodating.

At first sight, it may be difficult to see how anti-racism—the lobbying, policies, laws, and educational programs allegedly aimed at reducing racism and increasing equity—could in fact support racism and injustice. The aim of this book is to argue precisely this point and to attempt to elucidate the systemic motives behind "anti-racism". As such, a first working title for the book was "Against anti-racism".

Stated boldly, I advance the following radical principle.

The dogmatic theoretical position that the belief, attitude, or disposition of racism, the emotion of hate, and the action of violence are in themselves intolerable negatives, irrespective of the side in a conflict, irrespective of the degree of asymmetry of power in the conflict, and irrespective of the history of the conflict, is a position unambiguously in support of the real oppression from the dominant side.

Likewise, the unsubstantiated position that there is a likely benefit to society from systemic coercive pressures against racism of attitude, opinion, or belief, as surmised from the outward expressions of individuals, is a position that supports the racist dominance hierarchy that exploits society.

I argue that all such "anti-racism" anchored in institutional power supports the dominance hierarchy and that institutional (university, etc.) critical race theorists, knowingly or unknowingly, are instruments of the power establishment—are elite collaborators

---

associated with large scale trauma survival, arising from having "escaped" the harsh oppression that that comes from being black and of a low societal class. Malcolm X gives a vivid example of this phenomenon in his auto-biography, in the story of the young white college student who asks what she can do, only to be told, a la Freire, by Malcolm X that there is nothing she can do.

who are part of the anti-revolution or anti-liberation apparatus. Of course, there are exceptions that prove the rule, but if these exceptional individuals have not been removed then it is difficult to see how they are exceptions: the golden rule that institutions never work against themselves is virtually never broken.

"Anti-racism", as a policy project, is presented by its enthusiasts as logically deriving from an incontrovertible, indeed axiomatic, "truth": that racism of thought and opinion leads to racism of physical suppression and genocide; that preventing expression of racism (using the state apparatus or any other means) produces a less racist society. There is no historic or scientific evidence in support of this "truth". It appears to be based on the usual and incorrect conflation of correlation with cause; while selecting only a few examples that illustrate a positive correlation. I side with Malcolm X and others and argue the opposite, against this "truth". *A priori*, the odds are squarely on my side because in the great majority of correlations in social science a given correlation is due to a common cause rather than representing a causal relationship.

Broad proscriptions presented as deriving from what are alleged to be axiomatic truths (i.e., truths that need not be demonstrated) are a common social engineering device. Active state and corporate support for these campaigns are typically applied to the most dangerous truths about the system. A main example of such a dangerous truth is discussed in a following chapter: the dominant factor determining individual health is the direct bio-chemical impact of society's dominance hierarchy on the individual via one's immune system.

The latter "dangerous truth" about individual health, countered by the mega-lie engineered and maintained by establishment medicine (described below), may seem disconnected from the question of racism, but actually it is at the heart of how a dominance hierarchy is anchored on a primal level on our intrinsic human biology. Things are not as they appear. Even the things we believe about ourselves and our bodies are mostly wrong.

Denis G. Rancourt

Before embarking on a description of the biological foundation of hierarchical oppression, as a way to open a door to fresh thinking about racism, however, I start with concrete advice. I start with my experience of oppression in the university student environment, my (late) reaction to that oppression, and give my advice for fighting that oppression. This has a two-fold advantage compared to the usual formula of theory before practice. First, it connects the purpose of the book to my main expected audience of students and salaried professionals.[28] Second, it gives a sense of purpose to provide motivation for further reflection and analysis.

So, I start with my essay on the need for and practice of student liberation. The first reference there is the classic underground essay *The Student as Nigger* by Jerry Farber, which poignantly portrays the institutionalized oppression of students.[29]

For those who cling to hierarchies of oppression in relativizing the experiences of the oppressed, and who would argue that to even make a comparison between First World student oppression and Black slavery is to diminish the latter, I offer these words from Malcolm X:[30]

> *We have a common enemy. We have this in common: We have a common oppressor, a common exploiter, and a common discriminator. But once we all realize that we have this common enemy, then we unite on the basis of what we have in common. And what we have foremost in common is that enemy—the white man. He's an enemy to all of us. I know some of you*

---

[28] In the sense of Schmidt: *Disciplined Minds: A Critical Look at Salaried Professionals and the Soul-battering System That Shapes Their Lives*, Jeff Schmidt, Rowman & Littlefield Publishers, 2001.

[29] Farber, Jerry, *The Student as Nigger*, Contact Books, 1969.

[30] Malcolm X, *Message to the Grassroots*, speech, November 10, 1963, Detroit, Michigan.
http://www.sojust.net/speeches/malcolm_x_message.html

all think that some of them aren't enemies. Time will tell.

In this way, also, I start with the institutional origin of compliance in the modern society: School. In imposing its will on a captive population, the dominance hierarchy must first "educate". The education apparatus first aligns all workers, and then selects and indoctrinates the professional workers, while at the same time recruiting its elite collaborators.

The sequence of ideas is organized, in the book's chapters, roughly as follows:

❖ Need for and practice of student liberation;
❖ Dominance hierarchies are unavoidable in human societies;
❖ Institutions are naturally self-driven towards more control and dominance;
❖ The built-in constraint against runaway fascism is the individual's political impulse, and ability to creatively cooperate with other individuals to resist;
❖ The hierarchy continuously strives to both disorient and incapacitate the individual in order to maximize its growth in both size and depth;
❖ A main suppression mechanism against the individual is engineered guilt-based self-control anchored in self-image within one's community;
❖ North American "anti-racism" policy is one of several broad social manipulation instruments in a continuous systemic drive to incapacitate the individual;
❖ "Anti-racism" works by suppressing expression and disallowing overt inter-personal conflict needed for individual development, by providing a substitute for true anti-racism activism, by masking the mechanism of how actual liberation occurs, and by neutralizing attempts to out collaborators;

❖ "Anti-racism" supports racism of war and genocide by supporting a system which practices violent racist suppression on domestic and international fronts;

❖ The meaning of "house negro";

❖ Institutional behaviour rules that emerge;

❖ Respecting basic rights implies abolitionism.

The latter point sounds trivial but actually it is radical. There is a hierarchy-induced blindness which allows the opposite to be systematically applied in hierarchical society: basic rights are violated by the system under the pretext of defending the basic rights of more obedient subjects. In application, in the structure and logic of the "justice" system itself, it is clear that rights are hierarchically attributed by the dominance hierarchy, and that no other concept of "rights" can be tolerated by the system.

Need For and Practice Of Student Liberation

IN 2007, I wrote about a course I first offered in 2005, in an essay that has been widely re-published and whose original title was *Academic Squatting: A democratic method of curriculum development.*[31] The essay starts as:

> *I teach an activism course at the University of Ottawa.*
>
> *Not a course about altruism, volunteerism, charity, international aid or civic duty and building community within the confines of the status quo. But an activism course, about confronting authority and hierarchical structures directly or through defiant or non-subordinate assertion in order to democratize power in the workplace, at school, and in society.*

The essay has been cited repeatedly by my former employer as, first, a reason that I should be disciplined, and, recently, a reason that even if I was wrongly fired, I should not be allowed back on campus.

---

[31] Rancourt, Denis, *Academic Squatting: A democratic method of curriculum development*, Our Schools Our Selves, V. 16 N. 3 (#87) Spring 2007, p. 105-109.

Denis G. Rancourt

In 2010, I was an invited contributor to the European Education Congress, Bochum, Germany, an international conference entirely organized by students and funded by the European Union. There, I led two popular and intense sessions about student liberation. This prompted me to write the following essay for which I came to perceive a true need.

Student Liberation

The modern middle-class First World school and university systems are violently repressive[32]. These institutions are designed for replication and obedience training and rob the student of her natural thrust for independent inquiry, free expression, natural influence, and zeal for life[33].

Using the pretext that technical training requires "discipline" (read: mindless repetition) and "standardization" (read: demonstration of loyalty to imposed doctrine), the institutions of "higher learning" impose a regime of obedience training followed by professional and graduate school indoctrination[34].

The obedience training and whole-person neutralization is accomplished by strict and artificial disciplinal divisions, an authoritative classroom structure, an imposed unnaturally partitioned time use, unreasonable and repeatedly sequenced production deadlines (for assignments, tests, reports, examinations, etc.) that do not allow time to think, rank ordering of students to produce competition, a continuous administration of punishment and reward via grading and accreditation steps, isolation of the student where sharing and cooperation are cast as "cheating", normalization of

---

[32] Farber, Jerry, *The Student as Nigger*, Contact Books, 1969.

[33] Freire, Paulo, *Pedagogy of the Oppressed*, 1970; Continuum, NY, 2000.

[34] Schmidt, Jeff, *Disciplined Minds: A Critical Look at Salaried Professionals and the Soul-battering System That Shapes Their Lives*, Rowman & Littlefield Publishers, 2001.

behaviour and opinion via imposed group think value judgments, liberal applications of double speak, and a myriad of other such methods—all constantly adjusted to the evolving cultural and local conditions.

After the student is broken down by the obedience training, she is ready for the high level indoctrination of graduate and professional schools. This is achieved by the sophisticated process described by Jeff Schmidt. The professional worker must accept, make hers and project the doctrine of her "chosen" profession, in order to participate in the management of the First World Empire.

The repression of the student is real and is violent. The school and university institutions are the greatest forces in the student's life. The outcome determines the economic and societal status of the graduate and this status in turn is the single most relevant (statistical) indicator of life expectancy and personal health (see discussions of individual health factors later in this volume, and references therein).

The violence is seen in student suicides and assaults, in the widespread use of prescription psycho-pharmaceuticals and their trafficking, in widespread apathy and cynicism, in isolationism and escapism, in the modern array of self-destructive behaviours, and in the apparent relative inability to bond and form community. The root of the violence is maybe best explained by Paulo Freire:

> *Any situation in which "A" objectively exploits "B" or hinders his and her pursuit of self-affirmation as a responsible person is one of oppression. Such a situation in itself constitutes violence even when sweetened by false generosity; because it interferes with the individual's ontological and historical vocation to be more fully human. With the establishment of a relationship of oppression, violence has already begun.*
>
> *If people, as historical beings necessarily engaged with other people in a movement of inquiry, did not*

> *control that movement, it would be (and is) a*
> *violation of their humanity. Any situation in which*
> *some individuals prevent others from engaging in the*
> *process of inquiry is one of violence. The means used*
> *are not important; to alienate human beings from*
> *their own decision-making is to change them into*
> *objects.*

There is therefore a need for student liberation.

But the first barrier, as explained by Freire, is that the slave does not recognize that she is a slave. "We need the master because he organizes the work, feeds us, protects us..." (see also Farber).

Activist students prefer to fight for reduced tuition fees to ensure access to the oppression and its rewards. The slave should not have to pay with her future life (student debt) for the privilege of serving the master—fair enough. Slaves want to be oppressed fairly. I have known many activist students to leave demonstrations, actions, and teach-ins, in order to hand in assignments for deadlines and to obediently return to an oppressive classroom on Monday morning after a weekend of "solidarity action".

What can the student do to liberate herself?

Following Freire, I have come to believe that the answer is praxis, the "praxis" of Freire. Only such action fighting one's own oppression, in a cycle of repeated action and reflection informed by the oppressor's backlash, leads to both a deepening understanding of the oppression and an exhilarating liberation. True solidarity in battle then arises from the coalescence of these individual revolts and builds the culture of resistance essential to any societal liberation.

At the heart of this praxis lies "authentic rebellion". In what is perhaps the most profound statement ever made about education and learning in a hierarchical society, Freire puts it this way:

> *If children reared in an atmosphere of lovelessness*
> *and oppression, children whose potency has been*

frustrated, do not manage during their youth to take the path of authentic rebellion, they will either drift into total indifference, alienated from reality by the authorities and the myths the latter have used to 'shape' them; or they may engage in forms of destructive action.

How does this look in practice? How does praxis start and develop?

Students already resist a lot. Resistance is widespread and takes many forms. "Work to rule" is common to the dismay of baffled teachers. Most students refuse to adopt an artificial interest in the horse shit downloaded on them in the guise of intellectual discourse and that will be "on the exam". Students know when they are being spoken to rather than engaged with. And what would it mean to engage when the other side has a gun to your head?

Students turn off and regurgitate on demand to appease the oppressor. Teachers see the result but must grade satisfactorily (with an emphasis on factory) rather than confront the system's generalized failure and their part in it. Actually, we must conclude that this universal outcome is a desired feature of the school factory[35]. It ensures apathy and compliance and guaranties suppression of participation.

In addition, students secretly (among themselves) ridicule and criticize the professor in a healthy expression of sanity-preserving resistance. Only at the higher levels of indoctrination, when the student emulates the teacher as role model, does this behaviour subside to be replaced with ass kissing adulation.

Students also make heroic attempts to sabotage the obedience training by challenging the deadlines, workloads, grading schemes, work conditions, and atomization. They individually and collectively

---

[35] Rancourt, D.G., *Canadian Education as an Impetus towards Fascism*, 2009 vol.1 issue.2 of JASTE (*Journal for Activist Science & Technology Education*), pages 68-77.

negotiate for extended deadlines, reduced production, mitigated punishments, etc. They challenge the isolation and imposed competition by forming workgroups and by sharing output—they find ways to cooperate with each other at the risk of being banished via the system's ultimate charge of "academic fraud". In the words of David F. Noble, "When did cooperation become cheating?"

More frightening are the students who are able to feign interest and self-indoctrinate and who aggressively defend the system by punishing dissidence in their colleagues. These students want their special efforts to be recognized, rewarded, and not questioned by alternative behaviours. They want to "excel" and aspire to joining the club.

All forms of resistance are healthy and preserving if the resister sees herself as resisting and acts in defiance of the oppressor rather than succumbing to negative self-talk and negative self-image along the lines of the oppressor's imposed ideology. Authentic rebellion is where it's at.

More direct and satisfying forms of rebellion, with greater potential to empower the resister, might include speaking out in class to question aspects of imposed discipline, such as the deadlines, grading scheme, relevance of the material, imposed methods, disciplinal perspectives, etc.

Such direct interventions have the benefit that the teacher will react and thereby inform the class about real aspects of the system that it would be impossible to learn otherwise. Professors will show their true colours. The students will see them deflect, misinterpret, quash, impose, negotiate, etc.; a highly instructive experience.

Start small and see if you want to push it a little further. Ask to clarify the professor's response. Maybe ask, "Why not?" Maybe state that you do not understand the reasons given? See which colleagues side with you after class or express similar questions or opinions during class. Build on that support by developing ties with potential supporters and co-resisters.

Never accept overt intimidation or abuse from the professor.

Stand your ground in such violent attempts to repress your agency in the classroom. Explain the nature of the unacceptable behaviour and request an apology. Do this either privately with a witness or publicly in the classroom. If the potential for escalation of the repression exists, consider using modern technology to voice record the encounter for your protection. Such recordings of conversations that you are party to can be done secretly and are not illegal. No one needs to know and you have the benefit of knowing that you have physical proof if you ever need it for protection.

Only you can decide how far to go and how much to risk. The main point is that the lesson NOT be that you are powerless and must be subservient. Find a way for the lesson to be that you have power and can defend yourself. Find a way to win. The victory is not necessarily a policy change but rather your liberation.

In finding a way to win, consider that making things public and exposing the institution's in-class behaviour is a powerful way to both exert influence and protect yourself from further reprisals. Consider a blog and speaking to the student media or distributing flyers, etc.

A formal complaint to hierarchical authorities can also be useful, in that it will allow you to press further to expose mechanisms of institutional cover up and will show that you are not to be messed with. Keep your head up high knowing that you are right, that the violence against you is illegitimate, and that you need not fear the thugs that enforce the slavery from which you seek liberation.

You can always come back into the fold and power will be relieved to take you back in. This can be a good way to rest, reflect, and regroup, as you plan your continued liberation.

Eventually, you may find allies that will allow you to practice "academic squatting" of an entire class[36]. I have found this practice to be highly rewarding, even life-changing.

---

[36] Rancourt, Denis, *Academic Squatting: A democratic method of curriculum development*, Our Schools Our Selves, V. 16 N. 3 (#87) Spring 2007, p. 105-109.

If the professor is not an ally, groups of students can consider "academic hijacking" of credit courses in which a professor is told how it is going to be and that he can either stay and participate or leave.

Students with squatting and hijacking experience have what it takes to impose reforms on the curriculum. And liberated students are independent thinkers that do not practice immoral exploitations of others. They continue their liberation into the workplace.

Such a program of liberation activism is consistent with Paulo Freire's much repeated mantra that one can ONLY fight one's own oppression. Individuals that accept their own oppression cannot help liberate others. They only replicate, defend, and adjust the hierarchy of oppression that they inhabit.

I wish you a joyful and intense liberation full of self discovery and learning. Kick ass. Don't kiss ass.

Human Biology is Such that People Make and Inhabit Dominance Hierarchies[37]

NO CHARACTERISTIC OF human societies is more evident or defining than the fact that human societies are hierarchical. Groups of humans spontaneously form hierarchies. This truth is as self-evident as the statement that humans are social animals.

Here, I propose a known biological process present in animals including humans as a mechanism that drives spontaneous development of human dominance hierarchies. This explains the prevalence of hierarchies and their dominance focus in human societies.

In the following sections, I describe how growing hierarchical dominance is kept in check via a constant conflict between the aggressive impositions of the control structure and the natural political impulse of the individual for control and influence over his/her social environment.

Regarding our societal organizations, we like to nurture a species self-image where we are radically different from ants and bees. The idea goes like this. Ants and bees are automatons

---

[37] This chapter is partly taken from an article entitled *A Theory of Chronic Pain—a social and evolutionary theory of human disease and chronic pain* first published on the author's "Activist Teacher" blog on December 20, 2011.

completely governed by chemical and physical signals and each individual in the colony has its place which determines its physical body characteristics, adapted to the function of its class.

We distinguish these colony insects from mammals which we project have much higher degrees of individuality. We like to think of herds or packs of mammals as individuals who "choose" to come together and cooperate with each other. We generally don't admit body characteristics of individuals as being associated with class in societal dominance hierarchies.

But humans, primates and ants and bees may be much closer than we care to admit, then we are easily able to perceive.

There is an area of scientific research which points to just how wrong we may be. It is the study of the effects of a dominance hierarchy on the health of the individual. It turns out that in mammals and birds, for example, the health of the individual, barring accidents of nature, is primarily due to the individual's position in the society's dominance hierarchy[38][39][40]. Here, one needs to stress "primarily", as in by far the greatest determining factor—having a direct bio-chemical and physiological impact.

The dominance hierarchy in packs of monkeys, for example, determines fertility, resistance to disease, vigour, and longevity of the individual.

Now the dominance hierarchy as individual health determinant discovery is a paradigm-establishing discovery in medicine (if

---

[38] *The influence of social hierarchy on primate health,* Review, Robert M. Sapolsky, Science, vol.308, p.648-652, 2005. (and references therein) http://www.sciencemag.org/content/308/5722/648.abstract

[39] *Anti-smoking culture is harmful to health—On the truth problem of public health management*, Denis G. Rancourt, 2011. http://activistteacher.blogspot.com/2011/04/anti-smoking-culture-is-harmful-to.html

[40] *Is establishment medicine an injurious scam?*, Denis G. Rancourt, 2011. http://activistteacher.blogspot.com/2011/11/is-establishment-medicine-injurious.html

medicine is ever able to recognize it!), akin to plate tectonics in the Earth sciences, Newtonian mechanics in physics and evolution in biology, but it naturally leads to a follow-up question: Why?

Is there an evolutionary advantage, for mammals say, to suffer severe individual health effects from the intra-species dominance hierarchy? Otherwise, how has individual health vulnerability to dominance hierarchy survived on the evolutionary time scale? Is there a use or a need for individual health vulnerability to dominance hierarchy in terms of species survival, or is it simply a remnant of pre-insect-divide or colony-forming cells evolution?

A first glance would suggest that the human species, for example, cannot possibly benefit from having individual health materially and negatively affected by society's dominance hierarchy. But is this the correct conclusion?

I think not.

What is the most successful nervous-system-bearing animal species on Earth, in terms of both number of individuals and total biomass, and in terms of its transformative impact on the biosphere? Answer: Ants[41]. And the most successful large mammal? Humans[42]. Both live in highly hierarchical societies.

What is the sustaining biology of a highly hierarchical society of mammals? The individual must accept his/her place. All-out competitiveness of equal individuals (like a bar fight) is a recipe for disaster and does not lead to a highly stratified hierarchy. Pumped individuals who are and feel equally strong do not spontaneously

---

[41] *Is the burning of fossil fuel a significant planetary activity?,* Denis G. Rancourt, 2010.
http://activistteacher.blogspot.com/2010/08/is-burning-of-fossil-fuel-significant.html

[42] *Collective intelligence does not imply individual intelligence—Technology does not come from geniuses,* Denis G. Rancourt, 2011.
http://activistteacher.blogspot.com/2011/11/collective-intelligence-does-not-imply.html

organize into a stratified dominance hierarchy.

The built-in individual health vulnerability to dominance hierarchy is the biological (bio-chemical-metabolic) mechanism that sustains a positive feedback able to spontaneously generate a highly stratified dominance hierarchy.

If you are and feel sick from being dominated, you are not going to fight back. You are going to accept your place. The species is happy to have hoards of unhealthy individuals who will die young having spent their days doing the grunt work. What better way to stratify a successful species?

The impact on individual health also plays another key role, in addition to providing the feedback for stratification. It provides a needed mechanism of self-destruction for individuals who grow out or fall out of docility and compliance.

In a highly stratified society, individuals who cannot function must be eliminated, or they become a destructive force against the hierarchy. The police and jails would never be enough to achieve this without the built-in individual health vulnerability to dominance hierarchy.

As soon as the individual wants out and senses that there is no out, the individual self-destructs—rather than go on a destructive rampage, most of the time. This is called cancer and heart disease. It prevents the destructive rampage of the disillusioned individual and provides a natural end at the completion of the individual's cycle of utility to the hierarchy, to the species.

No wonder anarchists are so few and far between! But as with any positive feedback-driven system, it is inherently unstable[43].

In conclusion, the main bio-chemical determinant of individual health liability is one where the direct effects of society's dominance

---

[43] *Institutions build hierarchy between politico-cultural re-normalizations,* Denis G. Rancourt, 2011.
http://activistteacher.blogspot.com/2011/11/institutions-build-hierarchy-between.html

hierarchy on the individual's metabolism enable persistence, resilience, and continued development of the dominance hierarchy. There is a strong bio-chemical positive feedback, involving individual health, which drives the development of dominance hierarchy.

Put simply: the boss makes and keeps you sick such that you are less able to resist his/her excesses. He rewards and promotes you, and that makes you less sick, to the extent that you are able to serve him/her.

Denis G. Rancourt

Institutions Naturally Evolve Toward More Control

THIS CHAPTER CONTAINS three essays that present facets of the idea that institutions and society's structure as a whole evolve following a natural evolution model in which there is a driving force both to occupy more horizontal territory and to acquire more vertical depth of internal control. In the language of hierarchical imagery on a shrinking planet, the hierarchical pyramid, of global finance and militarization say, both sharpens by increasing its height to base ratio and increases its base on the planet.

The latter growth is akin to natural evolution where the only setbacks for an advantaged colony-forming species are accidental setbacks such as developing a vulnerability to a new parasite or disease, or not being able to adapt to sudden changes in environmental conditions, or losing ground to an internal break-off group arising from a learned advantage or mutation, and so on.

The defining challenge for society's dominance hierarchy, acting as a living organism, is the management of the individual which must be constantly shaped to function within the structure while sacrificing much of his or her internal drive for creative and free influence and participation. Therefore, there is a constant grooming campaign against individual impulses and freedoms.

Every once in a while, individuals coalesce within groups to regain some local control or to redefine their relation to the power structure to some degree. Less often, there is a broader revolution and much of the apparatus is "reset" with a new initial contract of understanding with the individual. From that point, the relentless march towards increased control over the individual starts again.

The individual which frustrates or impedes hierarchical development is seen as a malfunction needing to be either realigned or eliminated. The hierarchy's immune system against these deviant elements is the control, punishment, and incarceration apparatus, whether it be the police or another "social service". Capitalist society seeks to use individual impulses towards its aims. It has perfected an illusion of independence that feeds an artificial individual motivation, thereby providing some vitality to the whole. All individuals participate consistently with their positive or negative self-images which, in turn, are tied to their places within the hierarchy.

Here are three essays that reflect these ideas about societal evolution.

Institutions Build Hierarchy Between Politico-Cultural Re-Normalizations[44]

In the steady state of a society, in the absence of large direct consequences of war at home, including civil war and class war, in the absence of believable threats of violence against the dominance hierarchy, there are viable institutions which all continuously and progressively act to strengthen the dominance hierarchy.

The institutions are meant to maintain order and to provide stability for and continuity of the dominance hierarchy; by eliminating, deflecting, and consuming all threats. This is done under the pretense of educating, protecting, and providing for the obedient subjects of the dominance hierarchy.

---

[44] First published on the *Activist Teacher* blog, November 2011.

Denis G. Rancourt

The professionals who run all institutions are embedded into the overarching societal dominance hierarchy and must serve this master in order to maintain their status and relative privileges. Despite the solemn institutional mission-statement verbiage, therefore, these professionals know—for their own good—who they really serve.

As a result, the institutions grow and develop policies, practices and structures that monotonously sharpen and perfect the hierarchical pyramid.

The illusory "foundational principles" of institutions are merely the comforting promises which deceive subjects into abandoning autonomy in favour of accepting paternalistic management, and hierarchical control.

In advancing hierarchy (corporate fascism) the institutions necessarily erode the appearance of their own needed illusory "foundational principles" and must hide this erosion with ever more complicated or obtuse verbiage and ever more detailed and convoluted policies and rules; in exercises of sophistry that equal the most awe-inspiring human achievements (e.g., read Supreme Court rulings and note what is not said).

The subjects must be "educated" to receive this sophistry as high expert knowledge, even as the "foundational principles" telescopically disappear in reality.

In this way, the institutions (education, justice, health, finance, war, etc.) work together—in a highly coordinated fashion—to optimally support the dominance hierarchy. Jurisdictions are established, sequences of treatment enacted, etc.

The entire excise of law-making is an exercise in institution management and optimization to best serve and advantage the top strata of the dominance hierarchy.

And then, every once in a while, when circumstances in the bottom strata get too tense and the subjects start to see beyond the verbiage and expert management, things heat up and there may be adjustments, even re-normalizations, and we start somewhat refreshed, with clarified mission statements and so on.

And, following this jog or even back-step, "progress" can once again be pursued.

Such is the dance of institutional change as I see it.

The above theory of institutional change is predictive.

For example, since the institution's "foundational principles" pronouncements are a description of falsely promised repairs to damage necessarily caused by the dominance hierarchy and since the institution truly functions to support the dominance hierarchy, it follows that an institution will always work to distance itself from its own "foundational principles" and, where the stated "principles" give rise to strongly expressed expectations among the objectified subjects[45], to weaken ("re-define", "improve", "modernize", "clarify") its mission promises to the extent that it can.

The institution, therefore, works exactly to oppose its own "foundational principles" or purpose or mission statements because these statements are an expression of the targeted systemic consequences of hierarchy that the particular institution is meant to neutralize by subterfuge. The institution as substitute parent acknowledges the injustice, reassuringly states that the harm will be repaired via a fair (although complex) process, and sends the victim of hierarchy down a road with no issue; thereby cooling the mark out[46], causing the victim to invest in the false solution, and dissipating the complaint.

Another predicted consequence is that, for many individual professionals who work in institutions, there will be an unresolved dichotomy between elements of the individual's formal education regarding the benevolence of institutions and the dominant professional training culture of kissing ass to serve hierarchy and one's career "advancement." This, in turn, gives rise to the phenomenon of whistleblowers and their persecution and, depending

---

[45] Freire, Paulo, *Pedagogy of the Oppressed*, 1970.
[46] Goffman, Erving. *Cooling the Mark Out: Some Aspects of Adaptation to Failure*, Psychiatry Vol. XV: 451-63. 1952.

on the degree of social integration of the professional culture, to the phenomenon of professional worker malaise.[47] Otherwise, cynicism and peer-group-identification are major outlets.

Individual Freedom versus Collective Oppression as the Determinative Conflict in a Hierarchical Society[48]

There is no denying the first reality about humans. We are social beings, first and foremost regarding the forces that determine our lives. Our societies are hierarchical and, when not constrained by geography or balancing natural forces, spontaneously grow in size towards more hierarchy and fascism.

A recent antidote against the runaway excesses of Western monarchical and religious hierarchies has been the development of an ethos of individual freedom, spawned in the Enlightenment and anchored in mid-layer economic independence from the top hierarchical predators.

Enlightenment teachings were immediately integrated within the state apparatus of dominant powers; most notably in Prussia which also developed a first and most effective public education indoctrination system, on which all public education systems were quickly modeled.

These are manifestations of the first law of modern Western sustained hierarchies: The system strives to optimize an effective use of potent individual motivation while simultaneously striving for growth in size and more hierarchical control.

The anarchic thrust of self is society's primal motive force and hierarchical society is the main attenuator and destructor of self. Such

---

[47] Schmidt, Jeff. *Disciplined Minds: A critical look at salaried professionals and the soul-battering system that shapes their lives*, 2000.

[48] First published on the *Activist Teacher* blog, August 2011.

is the defining internal battleground of the modern hierarchy-on-steroids, otherwise known as the "free and democratic society".

Society offers the individual an identity within its structure, an identity that cannot be refused. The only alternatives are escape to a competing hierarchical society or physical death.

The most advanced modern systems of control that realistically vie for global dominance minimize internal threats by offering—to a chosen needed replicating sector (the middle and working classes)—an energetically sustained and constantly evolving illusion of individual "freedom", within an accompanying illusion of "reasonable" bounds on freedom. All others are expendable and are eliminated. The hierarchy has strong motive to eliminate all who do not readily accept the imposed personal identity; rather than maintain or attempt to integrate such threatening and ideologically-polluted sectors (aboriginals, economic apartheid survivors, etc.).

The illusion must minimally include regular occasions for release, at least moderately positive self-image within the hierarchy, and biological reproduction or an acceptable substitute. Compliance is also professionally managed using psychopharmacology (establishment medicine, etc.), and is constantly maintained by the mental environment and indoctrination industries (media, education, etc.). The system adds a widespread illusion of potential for personal advancement and meaning and rewards for particularly dedicated service (managing others).

That is society as it would be obvious to any outside observer, as obvious as when we observe a bee hive, an ant hill, a bird colony, or a pack of mammals. And this, therefore, is my interpretive framework for providing critiques of society's landscape.

Denis G. Rancourt

Gradual Change Is Not Progress[49]

Finally, this essay illustrates an example of an interpretative paradigm among professional workers and intellectuals who maintain the system by damping out emerging ideas of change. Here, I coined the term "service intellectual" which I had not seen being previously applied.

Comfortable First World liberal and left intellectuals claiming to work for change often project the opinion that positive change is best achieved by incremental improvements, gradual progress, dialogue, and negotiations that acknowledge the legitimacy of the other side. They assert that confrontation is 'counter-productive'. There is an army of academics, managers, and professionals, who will argue this point quite strenuously. They are the service intellectuals.

Their job is to block any model that would involve people of the disadvantaged side actually demanding change in the structure that keeps them at the bottom. Instead, they promote a dialogue model in which the disadvantaged side enters into loaded and unwinable negotiations with players that hold all the cards. These negotiations ensure that institutional structures of inequity are reinforced rather than progressively dismantled.

The service intellectuals argue that the only alternative to gradual change via education and dialogue is all out revolution where all the leaders are killed and replaced by tyrants. They propose a binary landscape of change where one must choose between either the gradual evolution that they manage or civil war and its uncertain outcomes. They monitor attempts for change and intervene when the latter attempts are 'too confrontational' or 'too undiplomatic' or 'too aggressive' or 'too radical', implying that those guilty of such crimes risk pushing us towards a bloody carnage. They contrast the restraint that they promote, design and manoeuvre to chaos.

This fallacy is so ingrained in much of the First World middle

---

[49] First published at Global Research, May 3, 2006.

class that it has become part of our culture. Many of us are allergic to opinions, differences, arguments, political discussions, etc.

The truth is that there is a broad spectrum of possibilities between polite consultation and an armed revolution. The truth is that change requires confrontation. Change requires confrontation because we are not talking about a change in hairstyle; we are talking about changes that redistribute power and relative advantages between different groups and between undemocratically controlled entities (corporations, banks, institutions) and people.

One argument of service intellectuals is that we are all people, that mutual respect must prevail, that those on both sides want what is good for everyone and that both sides only need a chance to see this.

The latter is certainly the right working assumption in interpersonal relations between individuals, but what are the two sides in societal and political struggles? The two sides in societal change are: management and workers, corporations and citizens, ruling elite and ordinary people, developers and residents, investors and inhabitants, etc.

A manager representing a corporation cannot be abstracted into the shoes of one's next-door neighbour who wants to talk about repairing a shared fence. The manager wields power over employees and is backed by a corporation with political clout. The situation is highly asymmetric. She may be a good mother to her children and she may be on the boards of a dozen charity organizations, but all that is irrelevant.

This manager has a job to do and it's not a pretty one. It's about manipulating and exploiting people (workers and consumers) to maximize profits for investors. It's about making sure that those with money get more money, as much as can be extorted. Public pressure and organized resistance are the employee's only chance.

If you don't need to use force, if a polite discussion will do the job, then you are on the same side! You are collaborating. You are in a symbiotic relation. You collaborate with your peers; you fight your exploiters. You love your neighbour; you fight your oppressor. Your heart is the size of your fist.

It's so damn obvious that it's hard to recognize. Union officials that collaborate with employer executives are part of the same management elite. Professions that collaborate are part of the same system of exploitation or of inherited privilege, such as the medical establishment and big pharma. Where there is 'cooperation' there is relative advantage for both parties, relative to other groups. Where there is institutionalized asymmetry and injustice, only confrontation and forced adjustments can partially restore equitable distribution. It doesn't take a Ph.D....

Actually, it does take a Ph.D.: one must be indoctrinated by a sufficient amount of formal education to not see the obvious and to partake in the lie. Gradual change my ass. A true intellectual doesn't preach the religion of gradual change but instead steps out of the mental framework of privilege to defend those on the other side. A true intellectual helps the other side develop the tools it needs and does not participate in neutralizing defiance.

Change occurs when people risk as much as they need to. First World citizens have a responsibility to risk as much as they need to— to be as effective as possible. True intellectuals are impolite, unprofessional, uncollegial, inconsiderate, etc. in pushing the limits as far as they must. In the light of the crimes being perpetrated by our governments and our corporations and financial institutions, true intellectuals have no choice. The question is not "What is too far?" but rather "What is far enough?".

Respect for individuals as persons is distinct from attacking representatives of oppressive power structures. The representatives must be attacked as representatives, as strongly as is necessary. They must be attacked as individuals wielding illegitimate (undemocratically controlled) power that is used unjustly. One must assume that they can be intimidated, perturbed, educated, etc., and that our actions will either make them see the light or at least force them to back down. People enmeshed in a system and culture of power and privilege cannot be reasoned with from the other side of the divide without the reasoning being based on a real threat.

Polite discussions and orderly debates are fine between different segments of the ruling class arguing about how best to preserve and enhance their class dominance but social justice comes only out of risk and confrontation, organized resistance and mass movements.

True intellectuals speak truth to power[50]. True intellectuals expose power and say the obvious. True intellectuals side with the exploited and oppressed and are examples of defiance.

Service intellectuals maintain a mental environment that preserves privilege. Service intellectuals maintain intellectual discipline—constantly identifying, isolating, and neutralizing true intellectuals, however few there are.

---

[50] Said, Edward, *Representations of the Intellectual*, 1994; Vintage Books, NY, 1996.

Denis G. Rancourt

The Individual Must be Continuously Disoriented

IN A DOMINANCE hierarchy each stratum of the hierarchy both controls the lower stratum and is controlled by the upper stratum. Each group, therefore, is subjected to oppression. That is, the individuals in each group are constrained from having their own free paths of self-definition, exploration, and free creative expression of influence and participation.

The great sociologist Paulo Freire has explained that all such oppression against the individual's self-realisation in community is necessarily violent. Current scientific knowledge of the direct bio-chemical effects from the dominance hierarchy and sociological studies of suicide and self-harm, including the various chemical and behavioural evasions, certainly confirm Freire's rule that hierarchical confinement is necessarily violently oppressive.

The individual's survival instinct will therefore cause him or her to consider how this violence can be avoided or minimized and to explore how to escape the oppression. The responses are varied. The most common responses, largely determined by our immune system's vulnerability to dominance, are to accept and "adapt" and, failing that, to self-destruct. An often less common response is to resist and rebel.

The degree to which individuals resist and rebel is largely

83

cultural and psychological; and it can be subject to runaway effects where groups find benefit and meaning in sustained and creative resistance and rebellion. The system must therefore continuously disorient the individual in order to hide the "resist and rebel" option.

The battleground of this maintenance of a false model is one where a variety of methods are employed and continuously adjusted. At the institution and government levels this adjustment warfare is called policy and law making. Like the overall structure itself, policies and laws evolve towards a tighter and sharper hierarchy, while projecting an image of justice and security and while consuming all resistance efforts.

The main methods for deceiving the individual in his or her own perception are guilt-based and anchored in self-image. Self-image is fundamentally about perception, of both self and the outside world. The individual must be made to see the world either without possibility of freedom (the lower classes) or with false models of how freedom and fulfilment are attained in practice (the managerial and professional classes).

Once individuals decide that "something must be done" and that they are prepared to take risks to cause change, then the false models of how change can be produced in practice become vital to maintaining the oppressive super-structure. Divide and conquer methods and co-optation are key anti-liberation strategies, where the factions that cooperate with the hierarchy promote the false models, combined with fierce punishment for identified and isolated leaders that fight hierarchical encroachment.

Malcolm X was an exceptionally lucid resistance leader who saw through the false models and fought against the collaborators. He identified that in such battles, a first rule is to recognize and name one's true enemy and a second rule is that the enemy will not give you anything without a fight. He understood that the enemy at most offered partial and illusory integration in order to strengthen its control over the larger most oppressed populations (both domestic and abroad).

This chapter explores the battleground of the dominance hierarchy's fight against the individual. The next essay is about Malcolm X in contrast to integrated pseudo-resistance.

Roundabout as Conflict-Avoidance versus Malcolm X's Psychology of Liberation[51]

Here I introduce the general notion of "roundabout" as a mechanism of conflict avoidance used by privileged social justice activists. I then contrast this pseudo-liberation activism with the needed true liberation activism of Malcolm X, which I argue to be consistent with the model of liberation of Freire.

Pacifism as Pathology

The now familiar concept of "pacifism as pathology" was introduced by Ward Churchill as the central characteristic of First-World middleclass so-called social justice activism. Churchill argued from history that all liberations were leveraged through violence and proposed that pacifism as cowardice was pathology[52].

Gandhi stated that it was better to practice armed resistance than to use pacifism as an excuse for cowardice[53]. Both men (Churchill and Ghandi) saw acceptance of and self-justification for one's (legal or circumstantial) slavery as pathology.

Paulo Freire's work showed that all hierarchies, no matter how cushioned in comfort, are violent and oppressive and argued that we could only fight our own oppression—that "solidarity" meant standing side by side with those fighting our same oppression. Freire advanced that all liberations had to be rooted in and driven by the struggles of the oppressed themselves—no matter how

---

[51] This essay was first published on the *Activist Teacher* blog, August 2010.

[52] *Pacifism as Pathology*, Ward Churchill, 1986.

[53] *Resolving the Israel-Palestine Conflict: What we can learn from Gandhi*, Norman G. Finkelstein, 2009.

underprivileged—and that inter-social-class "solidarity" was insignificant and limited to rare individuals who joined in battle on the front lines[54].

Churchill concentrated on the use of pacifism as an excuse to avoid the needed direct confrontation with the oppressive system. He and others have deconstructed and exposed First World pacifism as avoidance; including mainstream life-style environmentalism, ecological or economic isolationism, love ideologies, and so on, when taken to be activisms in themselves.

The latter authors did not explore or describe the creative psychological strategies or mechanisms of individuals in adopting pacifism as an "action" plan. I explore these strategies of evasive action (roundabout) used by an activist-minded sector of concerned citizens. My goal is to provide a radical criticism aimed at dedicated anti-hierarchy (social justice) activists.

Example of Roundabout: Education and Progressive Legislation

Here is an example. A visible minority suffers racism. As a way of avoiding effective direct challenges to this racism, members of this visible minority ally themselves (in "solidarity") with privileged social justice activist whites in order to train the majority societal group away from overt racist behaviour using social engineering managed by the establishment—using sponsored "education" and progressive legislation.

As a result, a privileged class of educated and integrated whites become self-conscious about racist behaviour and self-censor their racist expression, the establishment strengthens its illusion of fairness, and the minority loses its ability and legitimacy to enact effective direct daily confrontations against now-more-covert racism.

A victim in this particular roundabout is the collaborating visible minority because it puts its efforts in collaborating and its hopes in

---

[54] *Pedagogy of the Oppressed*, Paulo Freire, 1970.

the social engineering rather than practicing its liberation. It denies itself praxis (in the sense of Freire) and instead integrates itself more fully with the oppressive dominant hierarchy, thereby becoming more oppressed and more of an oppressor. Other victims are the lower social class individuals of the visible minority who lose actual solidarity with the now more integrated higher social class individuals of the visible minority and who are saddled with a stronger establishment more able to deflect their legitimate and persistent interests.

The above described roundabout is common as a general model for any oppressed group in a "free and democratic" First World setting: women, queers, blacks, language or cultural minorities, working class, working poor, homeless, disabled, non-status, elderly, disease-infected, professional workers, students, migrant workers, colonized aboriginals, prisoners, consumers, wage earners, tenants, home owners, single fathers, single mothers, and so on.

The above example involves a social class divide of the oppressed group but the class divide is not an essential feature because the roundabout is equally effective when there is no underclass of the oppressed group.

The essential feature of this roundabout is that the collaboration with the establishment, with the hierarchical system of control, is a (conscious or unconscious) diversion, in terms of personal psychology and personal resource allocation, away from effective direct confrontations, away from the praxis of liberation and away from Freire's needed revolt and authentic rebellion.

The dominant group partner in this roundabout also avoids its own immediate oppressions, instead of its members practicing their own liberations. As a result of this dedicated exercise of avoidance, members of the dominant group partner in the roundabout are perpetually depressed, in search of "hope", and routinely experience "burn out" despite self-identifying as privileged. This is because the authentically concerned dominant group partners (as opposed to the cynical higher-hierarchical-level dominant group partners such as law and policy makers) are attempting to removed themselves from their own pain and have denied themselves any possibility of directly and effectively addressing their own everyday oppression.

Example of Roundabout: Organizing and Politics

Another example of roundabout is when a concerned and sensitized individual, often burdened with survival guilt associated with his/her relative privilege and damaged by institutionalization (school, work, etc.) against which he/she has no personal experience of effective resistance, identifies an injustice needing to be redressed and launches into "organizing" as a substitute for immediate and direct action, as a substitute for initiating a praxis of liberation focussed on one's own oppression.

This type of organizing is based on recruiting membership, education regarding the issues, building a growing pool of progressive opinion, and so on, but it guards itself against radical actions that would "scare off potential allies" and clings instead to the mythology of a critical mass of opinion as a motor for societal change[55] [56].

In contrast, organizing that supports liberation is driven by the need for efficient learning, protection, and power amplification in a group of individuals already joined in solidarity via their practices of liberation. It is an organizing that is an organic part of the praxis, not a holding pattern of risk and confrontation avoidance.

Example of Roundabout: Deferring Societal Agency

In another roundabout the concerned and sensitized individual makes a conscious decision to temporarily sacrifice himself/herself to fully integrate the system and to seek advancement within the hierarchy

---

[55] *On the racism and pathology of left progressive First-World activism*, Denis G. Rancourt, 2010.

[56] *The Activist Wars*, Denis G. Rancourt, 2009.

with the rationalization that he/she will be more able to make positive change once a sufficient degree of power and influence is achieved.

The nature of a hierarchy is of course such that this is impossible. The rare individuals who break free from the top layers are expelled from the establishment. The other climbers either serve the system astonishingly well or blame themselves for failure and drop out if they cannot sanely serve.

The sacrifice of willing integration is a large price to pay if the individual does not discover rebellion and creative anti-hierarchical sabotage as methods to change the system from within. Workers and students play the system to survive and their suffering is evident in absenteeism (both physical and mental), indifference, detachment, cynicism, escapism, self-destruction, and so on.

This process and these difficulties are described by Schmidt for the case of professional workers[57]. The same process regarding schooling is the story of our institutionalization into the hierarchy, into an economy controlled by concentrated power. In this sense, student liberation during the developmental years would be a most fertile ground for societal transformation[58]. This is why schools are guarded from outside influence and from ideological divergence as rigorously or more so than prisons[59].

Anytime the individual substitutes direct self-defence using his/her body, language, personal influence in community, and personal power—at school or at work—with some indirect or circuitous make-work near-zero-risk scheme that involves going along or convincing others to also not act, then the individual is practicing roundabout rather than liberation activism.

---

[57] *Disciplined Minds*, Jeff Schmidt, 2000.

[58] *Need for and Practice of Student Liberation*, Denis G. Rancourt, 2010.

[59] *The Student as Nigger*, Jerry Farber, 1969

Malcolm X on Liberation Psychology

The Black Panther Party (originally the Black Panther Party for Self-Defence) was founded in 1966, one year after the murder of Malcolm X. The spectre of such an organized and focussed resistance was the main concrete driving force which led to significant civil rights gains for blacks. The Black Panther Party was eliminated by the white state's (FBI) political assassination unit known as COINTELPRO which was also involved in the Malcolm X assassination. Today U.S. blacks disproportionately populate the lowest economic class, and U.S. prisons.

In the words of Rev. Albert Cleage[60]:

> *Malcolm X was tremendously important, beyond our comprehension today...Malcolm laid down certain basic principles that we can never forget. He changed the whole course. The first basic principle that Malcolm laid down that we can't forget is this: The white man is your enemy. That is a basic principle, we can't forget it. I don't care what else they drag in from wherever they drag it—remember one thing, Malcolm taught one truth: The white man is our enemy. We can't get away from it, and if we accept and understand that one basic truth, his life was not lived in vain. Because upon that one basic truth we can build a total philosophy, a total course of action for struggle. Because that was the basic confusion which distorted the lives of black people, which corrupted the movements of black people.*
>
> *He didn't just say it...he went out and he lived it. He asked for moments of confrontation. He said*

---

[60] *Myths about Malcolm X*, Rev. Albert Cleage, speech delivered in Detroit, February 24, 1967.

> *we have got to break our identification, we can't go through life identifying with the white man or his government.... We must break our identification with the enemy, we must confront him, and we must realize that conflict and violence are necessary parts of a struggle against an enemy—that is what he taught. Conflict, struggle, and violence are not to be avoided. Don't be afraid of them...*

This foundational principle, that in the hierarchical oppression of blacks your enemy is your enemy, can be generalized to any particular hierarchical oppression and to all oppressions by hierarchies.

The oppressor by nature is your enemy. You cannot collaborate with your enemy who is devoted to your oppression, and come out ahead. At best, you will be used and transformed into your enemy.

Malcolm X's psychology of liberation is one where you recognize that the oppressor is an enemy that you cannot integrate, where you know that this enemy can only be deterred by your strength and your willingness to defend yourself.

In this psychology, like in Freire's, you do not fight the enemy in order to replace him in a hierarchy. You fight for liberation, not for an opportunity to create your own system of oppression. But you fight. You understand that this is an enemy and that all hierarchies must violently oppress.

If it's not clear that you are oppressed or that your oppressor is your enemy, then not only are you trapped and confused but you also protect and serve the oppressor. And you act against all those who are oppressed by the oppressor. You collaborate with the oppressor.

One does not like to live during a time of war and one does not like to have enemies. But this is a time of war and you are harmed by the system, and denied your full humanity, as surely as the million directly killed in Iraq and as surely as those held in the open air prison, illegally maintained by Israel, known as Gaza.

Hierarchy and Free Expression in the Fight Against Racism

By not fighting your own oppression directly as an individual person you protect the same system that practices these war crimes. By not understanding in your pores that this system and those who sustain, protect, and project it are your enemy until they stop, by not understanding this, you are co-opted into collaborating and into denying yourself your own liberation.

You can't even start a praxis of liberation until you start to recognize the enemy. And you can't sustain the struggle without knowing who the enemy is and that he is the enemy.

There is an us and a them. You are oppressed and you have an oppressor. You are oppressed by a hierarchical system of oppression. You target where you can best defend yourself, where you will inflict the most punishment. Call it punitive justice.

As soon as you lose sight that you are dealing with an enemy, then you are part of the oppressor. All the internal and external forces will make every attempt to confuse you on this point and to buy or to force your cooperation. In particular, those who invest in roundabout will vehemently pressure and coerce you to follow them because you represent a threat to their psychological investment.

In conclusion, if I keep my individual personal agency, my direct ability to have influence, my direct bodily ability to defend myself against my oppressor understood to be my enemy, at the point of my strongest connection to my oppressor, then I will not partake in roundabout. I will have all my available resources for my praxis of liberation which will naturally include organizing and community.

In the next essays in this chapter I give further examples, beyond "you have no enemies; your oppressor is a person who loves you; best integrate and work from the inside; etc.", of how the dominance hierarchy must constantly maintain an array of false paradigms that serve to hide foundational truths about society, "dangerous truths" that could allow germination of heightened individual perception about needed changes.

Two main false paradigms actively maintained by the dominance structure are presented in the following segments and can be expressed as:

(1)   Your personal physical and psychological (whole) health difficulties are due to something other than the oppression from the dominance hierarchy; and

(2)   Nothing can be done to change one's circumstances; or the best that can be done is to go along, cooperate with authority, and integrate, in order to have "positive influence" and best contribute meaningfully.

Self-knowledge, about one's own body and one's power in society, must be made unachievable at all costs. The establishment's experts align perfectly to generate and maintain mega-lies about health and change, while constantly singing that personal fulfilment is the ultimate goal.

On the Smoke Screen of Public Health Lobbying[61]

We are all going to die from second-hand cigarette smoke on outdoor patios.

The medical profession agrees and the government allocates significant resources to negative propaganda and enforcement against smoking.

Ever wonder why these good folks are so concerned about our health? Are there much larger health risks that we never hear about? Are there systemic or societal reasons in the selection of those health risks targeted to be actively vilified by the establishment?

Fatty diets, smoking, sedentary lifestyle, car seat-belts, work safety...what do all these health and safety recommendations have in common? How do these risk factors compare to the real killers?

In Canada, according to government scientists, 85% of lung

---

[61] First published on the *Activist Teacher* blog, April, 2011.

cancers are due to smoking and lung cancer is the leading type of cancer deaths (one quarter of all cancer deaths).

This sounds like all smokers are going to die of lung cancer. In fact[62], if each and every individual in Canada smoked approximately one pack of cigarettes per day, then the resulting death rate from lung cancer would nonetheless be less than only two deaths per thousand inhabitants per year, less than twenty-percent or so of the death rate from all causes, and this would typically only kick-in after twenty to thirty years of such sustained smoking by the entire population.

Get a grip. Smoking is not going to cause extinction of the species.

This also means that most heavy smokers (say, two packs a day) will not die of lung cancer. More than eighty to ninety percent or so of heavy smokers will not die of lung cancer.

In addition, lung cancer rates in smokers are highly non-linear with amount smoked, such that a meaningful cancer risk cannot be attributed to light or occasional smokers. So paleeese stop having visions of your early lung cancer death when you trot by an outside smoker holding a "death stick".

Medical Error

Now why do so many heavy smokers not die of lung cancer? And why do other smokers get lung cancer? And why are fifteen percent or so of lung cancers not due to obvious causal agents? This may be related to the real killer that I am going to tell you about.

But before we talk about the real "natural" killer of people, let me remind the reader of the established fact that is virtually absent from establishment propaganda and establishment public health policy development: The third leading cause of death in North

---

62

http://en.wikipedia.org/wiki/File:Cancer_smoking_lung_cancer_correlation_from_NIH.svg

Denis G. Rancourt

America is medical error, after cardiac disease and cancer[63] [64].

This is an apropos reminder that establishment scientists are service intellectuals and that establishment medicine may have little to do with public health[65]. It is a reminder of just how much we may have been misled about the real dangers to our own bodies...

Anarchy as the Only Healthy Lifestyle

As it turns out, there is extensive and conclusive scientific research that simply does not get talked about in the controlled mental environment and that is virtually not taught in medical schools. This research shows that dominance hierarchies are the greatest impediments to human health in stable and "advanced" societies[66], excluding war and imposed deprivation; which also arise from dominance hierarchies.

The violence of human dominance hierarchies in our stable "advanced" societies is corroborated by documented empirical facts and experimental results establishing a dominant causal relationship between socioeconomic status and human health and mortality; which is not simply due to differences in resource allocation, access to medical care, life-style differences (smoking, drinking, diet, exercise, etc.), work accidents and other such relatively "incidental" whole-population factors, but which instead is due to the direct impacts of dominance hierarchy on physiological functions.

In a word, the boss makes you sick—whether you like him/her or not.

Socioeconomic status is the single most dominant predictor of

[63] *Is US Health Really the Best in the World?*, Barbara Starfield. Journal of the American Medical Association, Vol.284, No.4, 2000, pages 483-485.]
[64] *Health 'Care' in the United States*, Dr. Barbara Starfield interviewed on CHUO 89.1 FM Ottawa (Canada), The Train.
[65] *Some big lies of science*, Denis G. Rancourt, 2010.
[66] *The influence of social hierarchy on primate health*, Review, Robert M. Sapolsky, Science, vol.308, p.648-652, 2005. (and references therein)

health, and the physiological mechanisms for this causal relation (from socioeconomic status to individual health) are being elucidated by population studies and laboratory experiments.

The vector is psychosocial stress which significantly impacts the immune system, fertility, the brain (see below), the heart (hypertension, pathogenic cholesterol profile), and adrenal gland function. This is particularly relevant when we consider the canonical link between the immune system and cancer (second leading cause of death) and the fact that the first leading cause of death is cardiovascular failure.

The known main stress-causing social circumstances arising from dominance hierarchies are (see Sapolsky):

> *(i) low degrees of social control and predictability...;*
> *(ii) a paucity of outlets after exposure to stressors...;*
> *(iii) a paucity of social support...; or (iv) high rates*
> *of physical stressors...*

This explains why we seek protections via rules, laws, and regulations; why we seek outlets and social support; and why we avoid contacts with the hard end of the dominance hierarchy.

In addition, "subjective [socioeconomic status] can be at least as predictive of health as is objective [socioeconomic status]," meaning that one's self-perception as a subordinate individual in the dominance hierarchy can be as important as one's actual status. This in turn implies that culture and propaganda are significant public health factors in dominance hierarchies.

Public Health Cover Up

If this is the truth about health then the establishment has a truth problem. The establishment is dedicated to maintaining and benefiting from society's dominance hierarchy yet this hierarchy is bad for public health and quality of life.

The obvious solution is cover up. But the evidence is so

startling, so evident to even a neophyte observer of society that the cover up needs to be broad and sustained. It needs to involve every educational institution and professional school[67], every propaganda instrument, and every relevant management ministry.

> Indeed, the interests of the oppressors lie in 'changing the consciousness of the oppressed, not the situation which oppresses them' [Simone de Beauvoir]; for the more the oppressed can be led to adapt to that situation, the more easily they can be dominated. [68]

In such a cover up, like any cover up, one needs a proper patsy; or an array of diversions conveniently locked into our hierarchy-induced wants for protection and the reassurances that obedience will provide rewards.

The main diversion, therefore, is to invent or exaggerate health risks that can be reduced by personal lifestyle choices, by discipline and obedience. Of course those with the luxury of such lifestyle obedience are also of higher socioeconomic status, thereby providing a convenient false corroboration of the public health policy.

There be smoking. And trans-fat, and residual carcinogens, and flu shots, and heavy metals in urban drinking water, and cancer screening, and annual check-ups, etc. The violently debilitating dominance hierarchy is a given that cannot be examined (we can't even question the concepts of low corporate taxes and mobile capital) and all health problems are either accidental or related to lifestyle "choices" in a "free and democratic" society. Tadaaaa…

---

[67] *Disciplined Minds*, Jeff Schmidt, 2000.
[68] *Pedagogy of the Oppressed*, Paulo Freire, 1970.

It Makes You Stupid

Dominance hierarchy stress on the subordinate individual is directly a killer; and…it makes one stupid (Sapolsky):

> *Animals who are socially stressed by the dominance hierarchy for prolonged periods undergo neurobiological changes as well. This can involve inhibition of neurogenesis, dendritic atrophy, and impairment of synaptic plasticity in the hippocampus and altered patterns of apoptotic cell death (increases in the cortex and decreases in the hippocampus)*

Fortunately, there is a lifestyle practice that can make you smart (Freire):

> *But in the last analysis, it is the people themselves who are filed away through the lack of creativity, transformation, and knowledge in this (at best) misguided system [of education]. For apart from inquiry, apart from the praxis, individuals cannot be truly human. Knowledge emerges only through invention and re-invention, through the restless, impatient, continuing, hopeful inquiry human beings pursue in the world, with the world, and with each other.*

Here Freire's "praxis" means an authentically rebellious praxis of liberation anchored in a fervent dedication to fighting one's own oppression, against one's objectification[69][70][71].

---

[69] *Need for and Practice of Student Liberation*, essay, Denis G. Rancourt, 2010.

[70] *On the racism and pathology of left progressive First-World activism*, essay, Denis G. Rancourt, 2010.

Denis G. Rancourt

Is Establishment Medicine an Injurious Scam?[72]

Establishment medicine is sustained by a triad of core deceptions: (1) An apical lie by omission which does not admit that the predominant causal determinant of an individual's health is the individual's real and perceived place in the society's dominance hierarchy, (2) the "voodoo lie" of the false scientific foundation of its professional practice which does not admit that most of medical research used to justify the recommended "treatments" is wrong and that consequently the "treatments" are ineffective at best, and (3) the dirty secret that establishment medicine (in North America) is itself the third leading cause of death, after cancer and cardiovascular failures for which medicine is of little use. All three core deceptions have been decisively exposed by leading-edge mainstream researchers whose works have had virtually no impact in reforming the medical profession.

In his *An Appeal to the Young,* Peter Kropotkin, in 1880, challenged young graduates entering the professions this way[73]:

> *"What the devil!" you say. "But if abstract science is a luxury and practice of medicine mere chicane; if law spells injustice, and mechanical invention is but the means of robbery; if the school, at variance with the wisdom of the 'practical man,' is sure to be overcome; and art without the revolutionary idea can only degenerate, what remains for me to do?"*
>
> *Well, I will tell you.*

---

[71] *Roundabout as conflict-avoidance versus Malcolm X's psychology of liberation,* essay, Denis G. Rancourt, 2010.

[72] First published on the *Activist Teacher* blog, November 2011.

[73] *An Appeal to the Young,* Peter Kropotkin, 1880.
http://dwardmac.pitzer.edu/anarchist_archives/kropotkin/appealtoyoung
.html

> *A vast and most enthralling task; a work in*
> *which your actions will be in complete harmony with*
> *your conscience, an undertaking capable of rousing*
> *the noblest and most vigorous natures.*

Professional schools of course do not follow Kropotkin's curriculum. Instead, professional training directs the student's self-indoctrination to accept the scam of the profession[74].

Hierarchy, the Hidden Predominant Health Factor

To potential medical doctors Kropotkin prescribes this:

> *You, doctors…never weary of telling us today,*
> *tomorrow, onward to decay if men remain in the*
> *present conditions of existence and work; that all*
> *your medicaments must be powerless against disease*
> *while the majority of mankind vegetate in conditions*
> *absolutely contrary to those which science tells us are*
> *healthful; convince the people that it is the causes of*
> *disease which must be uprooted, and show us all what*
> *is necessary to remove them.*
>
> *Come with your scalpel and dissect for us, with*
> *an unerring hand, this society of ours, hastening to*
> *putrefaction. Tell us what a rational existence should*
> *and might be. Insist, as true surgeons, that a*
> *gangrenous limb must be amputated when it may*
> *poison the whole body.*

Non-"abstract" science has, since Kropotkin's time, further informed

---

[74] *Disciplined Minds: A critical look at salaried professionals and the soul-battering system that shapes their lives*, Jeff Schmidt, 2000. http://disciplinedminds.tripod.com/

us about the "conditions absolutely contrary to those which science tells us are healthful" as follows: Of course a lethal workplace (such as unregulated mining in a toxic dust environment) kills, as do starvation, malnutrition, hypothermia and dehydration, as extreme physiological stresses that cause metabolic failures or invite disease. But barring obvious utmost physical causes of health failure associated with war and extreme exploitation of populations, science has shown that the next predominant determinant (not just correlate but causal determinant) of individual health is the individual's real and self-perceived position in the society's dominance hierarchy[75] [76].

Documented empirical facts and experimental results from the small but vibrant "hierarchy and health" mainstream medical research community establish a dominant causal relationship between socioeconomic status and human health and mortality; which is not simply due to differences in resource allocation, access to medical care, life-style differences (smoking, drinking, diet, exercise, etc.), work accidents and other such relatively "incidental" whole-population factors but which instead is due to the direct impacts of dominance hierarchy on physiological functions.

As noted above, socioeconomic status is the single most dominant predictor of health, and several of the bio-physiological mechanisms for this *causal* relation (from socioeconomic status to individual health) have already been elucidated by population studies and laboratory experiments.

It follows, therefore, that one of the medical establishment's first priorities will be to keep this pivotal and conclusive scientific finding—that the society's dominance hierarchy is the dominant

---

[75] *The influence of social hierarchy on primate health*, review, Robert M. Sapolsky, Science, vol.308, p.648-652, 2005, and references therein. http://www.sciencemag.org/content/308/5722/648.abstract

[76] *Anti-smoking culture is harmful to health: On the truth problem of public health management*, Denis G. Rancourt, 2011.
http://activistteacher.blogspot.ca/2011/04/anti-smoking-culture-is-harmful-to.html

causal determinant of individual health—hidden from collective consciousness. Otherwise, Kropotkin's medical school curriculum might threaten to impose itself and the medical profession would be robbed of its placebo and poison-as-medication scams which are the economic drivers of its societal status, within the dominance hierarchy which causes ill-health in all but the uppermost strata in its structure....

That subservience kills—is THE killer, is a truth that must not surface.

Like with any profession, the medical profession's predation of the broader society is premised on a lie so big that the truth cannot easily emerge. Imagine that all the "health factors" that medicine preoccupies itself with are completely secondary, when they are relevant at all, compared to the overbearing impact of an individual's oppression from the society's dominance hierarchy.

As noted above, in addition to the dominance hierarchy stress on the subordinate individual being directly the main killer, it also directly makes one stupid, which may be part of the reason, in a stable dominance hierarchy, that corrupt and predatory professions and organizations are so resilient against exposure and reform—but I digress.

That subservience is the killer is the apical lie of the medical establishment. It is a lie by omission. Next there is the lie of a false practice, what might be called the "voodoo lie", that the mainstream practice of medicine is not based on science as alleged by adherents. And, finally, there is the dirty secret that medicine is the third leading cause of death in "advanced" societies (North America), surpassed only by conditions (cancer and heart disease) for which medicine can do virtually nothing. Let us examine these further lies as follows.

Medical Research—Bad Science

A small group of establishment so-called "meta-researchers" have pointed out what must at some level be obvious to many clinicians and researchers, that most medical research findings are wrong[77]. "80 percent of non-randomized studies (by far the most common type) turn out to be wrong", as do large fractions of both randomized and large randomized trials. Meta-researchers find that most medical research on which medical practice is based is "misleading, exaggerated, and flat out wrong."[78]

These meta-researchers are highly recognized and publish in the top medical journals,[79] [80] yet their message does not drive reforms in the profession. I have tentatively explained this paradox in this way[81]:

> [T]he medical establishment, with its heavy mythology about saving lives, is in deep need of reparative peer-group banter. And what better banter then that from a meta-researcher explaining that from a statistical perspective—without actually ever singling anyone out—that from a statistical perspective most of what we take as known and most

---

[77] Ioannidis, John PA, *Why Most Published Research Findings Are False*, 2005, PLoS Med 2(8): e124.
doi:10.1371/journal.pmed.0020124

[78] *Lies, Damned Lies, and Medical Science*, David H. Freedman, The Atlantic, 2010.
http://www.theatlantic.com/magazine/archive/2010/11/lies-damned-lies-and-medical-science/308269/

[79] Ioannidis, John PA et al., *Replication validity of genetic association studies*, Nature genetics, 2001, 29(3), 306-309.

[80] Ioannidis, John PA, *Contradicted and initially stronger effects in highly cited clinical research*, JAMA: the Journal of the American Medical Association, 2005, 294 (2), 218-228.

[81] [6] *On the sociology of medical meta-science: Exposing the Truth supports the Lie*, Denis G. Rancourt, 2011.
http://activistteacher.blogspot.ca/2011/11/on-sociology-of-medical-meta-science.html

> *of what we do is wrong, haha, see the graph over here...*
>
> *[The medical meta-researcher] is a provider of self-image-soothing locker-room banter for the medical profession. Only colleagues who will dare to point fingers have any chance of changing anything.*

In any case, the main point here is that most medical research is not reliable. This is not surprising for many reasons, both societal and scientific, not the least of which is that the research concerns itself with distant secondary or false causes of ill-health since it is blind by-design to the predominant direct causal factor that is the society's dominance hierarchy.

The research studies by-design exclude the most relevant interpretive paradigm (effects of hierarchical oppression) and instead concentrate on ancillary factors which in turn are statistically disordered by the particular circumstances of the hierarchical oppression and of the individual's response to this oppression.

The career-driven researcher attempts to extract (consequently dubious and always tenuous) statistical correlations between supposed causal indicators and supposed health indicators, both being neither, in view of recommending a treatment, which often happens to be an expensive pharmaceutical "medication" aimed at providing only a marginal improvement in patient comfort without an objective measure of patient comfort. The latter is called "palliative care".

So drugs are approved as demonstrated-safe and then withdrawn because they are killers and organs are removed as standard treatment until the practice "evolves" and regular cancer tests are highly recommended until they are "discovered" to do more harm than good and AIDS is created into a human epidemic thanks to vaccination programs and fat is unhealthy until it is declared healthy and poison is good for you because when we stop the poison you think you feel better than before we started and indicator symptoms (like high blood pressure) can be removed with powerful drugs so you can die of the actual cause with the benefits of drug side effects and without ever knowing why and on and on.

The practice of medicine, when it is based on scientific research, is based on bad research providing wrong results. Modern medicine is good at trauma intervention (heart attack, road accident, sporting accident, etc.). Beyond that: Beware. Beware indeed, as the next section shows.

Medical Practice—Death Machine

We've all heard some medical doctor interviewed on the radio gratuitously make the bold proposal that life expectancy has increased thanks to modern medicine. Nothing could be more distant from the truth.

Life expectancy has increased in First World countries thanks to a historical absence of civil and territorial wars, more accessible food, less work and non-work accidents, and better overall living and working conditions. Not surprisingly given the above discussion, the single known strongest documented indicator of personal health within and between countries is economy status, irrespective of access to medical technology and pharmaceuticals.

As noted above, the only statistically significant advances in establishment medicine (distinct from public health) are in trauma intervention. That is, less young folks in urban centers die of heart attacks and more car accident victims survive.

Outside of trauma intervention, the impact of establishment medicine is far from neutral. It is conclusively negative. The third leading cause of death in North America is medical error, after cardiac disease and cancer—not counting misattributed deaths from correctly administered "treatments" and there is a large gap between this conservative underestimate in the number of medical error deaths and the fourth leading cause of death.[82] [83] [84]

---

[82] *Is US Health Really the Best in the World?*, Barbara Starfield. Journal of the American Medical Association, Vol.284, No.4, 2000, pages 483-485.]

Since medicine can do little for heart disease and cancer and since medicine has only a small overall statistical positive impact in the area of trauma interventions, it is fair to conclude that public health would increase if all medical doctors simply disappeared[85].

And think of all the time loss and stress that sick folks would save....

One of the most dangerous places in society is the hospital. Medical errors include misdiagnoses, bad prescriptions, prescriptions of medications that should not be combined, unnecessary surgery, unnecessary or badly administered treatments including chemotherapy, radiation treatment, and corrective surgeries.

In a remarkable disregard for logic and for discriminating cause and ancillary effect, doctors in their recommended practice prescribe drugs to remove symptoms that are risk indicators (i.e., correlates) rather than address the causes of the risks, thereby only adding to the assault on the body.

Bonehead medical doctors and psychiatrists routinely apply unproven (see above) "recommended treatments" and prescribe dangerous drugs for everything from high blood pressure from a sedentary lifestyle in oppression, to apathy at school, to anxiety in public places, to post-adolescence erectile function, to non-conventional sleep patterns, and to all the side effects from the latter drugs.

Psychiatry's large-scale vicious attack against people is documented in the works of Peter Breggin[86] who explains how this

---

http://jama.jamanetwork.com/article.aspx?articleid=192908

[83] *Health 'Care' in the United States*, Dr. Barbara Starfield interviewed on CHUO 89.1 FM Ottawa (Canada), The Train.
http://trainradio.blogspot.ca/2010/01/health-care-in-united-states.html

[84] Graedon, J. and Graedon, T., *Top Screwups Doctors Make and How to Avoid Them*, 2012, Three Rivers Press.

[85] *Some Big Lies of Science*, Denis G. Rancourt, 2010.
http://activistteacher.blogspot.ca/2010/06/some-big-lies-of-science.html

[86] Several books by Peter Breggin. For example, *Toxic Psychiatry*, 1991; and

profession has in the recent past gone along with institutionalized mass murder[87].

Medical Predators

We must conclude that establishment medicine, anchored in the medical profession, is an injurious scam and an occupying predator of people constrained within society's dominance hierarchy. Of course doctors are respectable members of society, good parents, responsible professionals and all that but they are also the professional maintainers and executors, conscious or not, interested or not, of a system of exploitation and deceit that drains resources and vitality from an occupied population.

In light of the above, it is difficult to accept that "progressive" elements of society such as national workers unions in Canada, would campaign in favour of a universal drug program, for example, rather than directly campaign for health sanity and stringent constraints against big-pharma and medical insurance corporations and their political influence.

A Left that stabilizes the dominance hierarchy rather than attempts to flatten it (democratize it) is part of the problem. At least on the libertarian Right, individuals seek a free hand in defending themselves.[88]

"Lies, lies, lies" is the norm regarding anything important that could lead to self-knowledge. The next essay shows how the scientific and technocratic professions spontaneous participate in the web of lies that maintain "order", while deriving obvious advantage from their roles.

Brain-Disabling Treatments in Psychiatry, 2008. http://www.breggin.com/

[87] Video of conference talk by Peter Breggin, *The Violence Initiative*, 2010. http://youtu.be/MQZdUmxG1Es

[88] *Denis Rancourt on anti-hierarchy activism*, Nine-part video mini-series, Denis G. Rancourt, 2010. http://activistteacher.blogspot.ca/2010/09/denis-rancourt-on-anti-hierarchy.html

Some Big Lies of Money, Medicine, and Environmental Science[89]

> *[T]he majority of politicians, on the evidence available to us, are interested not in truth but in power and in the maintenance of that power. To maintain that power it is essential that people remain in ignorance, that they live in ignorance of the truth, even the truth of their own lives. What surrounds us therefore is a vast tapestry of lies, upon which we feed.*
>
> —*Harold Pinter, Nobel Lecture (Literature), 2005*

The maintenance of the hierarchical structures that control our lives depends on Pinter's "vast tapestry of lies upon which we feed." Therefore the main institutions that embed us into the hierarchy, such as schools, universities, and mass media and entertainment corporations, have a primary function to create and maintain this tapestry. This includes establishment scientists and all service intellectuals in charge of "interpreting" reality.

In fact, the scientists and "experts" *define* reality in order to bring it into conformation with the always-adapting dominant mental tapestry of the moment. They also invent and build new branches of the tapestry that serve specific power groups by providing new avenues of exploitation. These high priests are rewarded with high class status.

The Money Lie

The economists are a most significant example. It is probably not an accident that in the United States at the end of the nineteenth century the economists were the first professional analysts to be "broken in",

---

[89] This essay was first published on the *Activist Teacher* blog, June 2010; and also in NEXUS, Oct-Nov 2010 issue, pages 39-42 & 82.

in a battle that defined the limits of academic freedom in universities. The academic system would from that point on impose a strict operational separation between inquiry and theorizing as acceptable and social reform as unacceptable.[90]

Any academic wishing to preserve her position understood what this meant. As a side product, academics became virtuosos at nurturing a self-image of importance despite this fatal limitation on their societal relevance, with verbiage such as: the truth is our most powerful weapon, the pen is mightier than the sword, a good idea can change the world, reason will take us out of darkness, etc.

So the enterprise of economics became devoted to masking the lie about money. Bad lending practice, price fixing and monopolistic controls were the main threats to the natural justice of a free market, and occurred only as errors in a mostly self-regulating system that could be moderated via adjustments of interest rates and other "safeguards."

Meanwhile no mainstream economic theory makes any mention of the fact that money itself is created wholesale in a fractional reserve banking system owned by secret private interests given a licence to fabricate and deliver debt that must be paid back (with interest) from the real economy, thereby continuously concentrating ownership and power over all local and regional economies.

The rest of us have to earn money rather than simply fabricate it and we never own more when we die. The middle class either pays rent or a mortgage. Wage slavery is perpetuated and degraded in stable areas and installed in its most vicious varieties in all newly conquered territories.

It is quite remarkable that the largest exploitation scam (private money creation as debt[91]) ever enacted and applied to the entire

---

[90] *No Ivory Tower: McCarthyism & the Universities*, Ellen W. Schrecker, Oxford University Press, 1986.
[91] Grignon, Paul, *Money as Debt*,
http://video.google.ca/videoplay?docid=5352106773770802849

planet does not figure in economic theories.

Economists are so busy modeling the ups and downs of profits, returns, employment figures, stock values, and the benefits of mergers for mid-level exploiters that they don't notice their avoidance of the foundational elements. They model the construction schedule while refusing to acknowledge that the terrain is an earthquake zone with vultures circling overhead.

Meanwhile the financiers write and re-write the rules themselves and again this process does not figure in macroeconomic theories. The only human element that economists consider in their "predictive" mathematical models is low-level consumer behaviour, not high-level system manipulation. Corruption is the norm yet it does not figure. The economies, cultures and infrastructures of nations are wilfully destroyed in order to enslave via new and larger national debts for generations into the future while economists forecast alleged catastrophic consequences of defaulting on these debts....

Management tools for the bosses and smoke and mirrors for the rest of us—thank you, expert economists.

The Medicine is Health Lie

That "medicine is health" is a mega-lie should be abundantly clear from the above discussion in this chapter: Establishment medicine does far more harm than good—it's a mass killer; medical research is a hoax perpetrated by careerist researchers and the chemical-bio-pharmaceutical industrial cartel; and the dominant causal agent attacking individual health is the dominance hierarchy and its direct psycho-biological impact on the immune system and vital functions.

Medical doctors participate in the crime of establishment medicine because their indoctrination, via the concentration camp methods described by Schmidt[92], is so effective, and because their

---

[92] Schmidt, Jeff, *Disciplined Minds: A Critical Look at Salaried Professionals and the Soul-battering System That Shapes Their Lives*, Rowman & Littlefield

Denis G. Rancourt

maintained status within the social hierarchy depends on their willing collaboration—a status which, in turn, is intimately tied to and largely defines the collaborator's self-image.

The gruesome history of psychiatry[93] and its enthusiastic collaboration with the criminal Nazi social project is an example that is not in fact, in terms of magnitude of human suffering, more egregious than the present large scale torture and murder of subjects by the modern medical establishment, in combination with the institutions of physical and chemical containment applied to adults, the elderly, and children.

The lie extends to the myth that MDs and medical researchers anywhere near understand the human body. And the latter well-guarded lie encourages us to put our faith in doctors, thereby opening the door to a well-orchestrated profit bonanza for big pharma. Much of our trust in doctors is also a consequence of hierarchy, rather than a rational individual choice, since hierarchy imposes a psychology of paternalism, dependency, and victimhood among its subjects.

As a practical example illustrating the lie of maintenance medicine, the first thing that Doctors Without Borders (MSF) volunteers need to do in order to contribute significantly in disaster zones is to "forget their medical training" and get to work on the priority tasks at hand: water, food, shelter, and disease propagation prevention; not vaccinating, or operating, or prescribing medication…public health comes from safety, stability, social justice, and economic buying power, not MRI (magnetic resonance imaging) units and prescription drugs.

It's unbelievable the number that medicine has done on us; it's just one more way to keep us stupid (ignorant about our own bodies) and artificially dependent on the control hierarchy. Economically disadvantaged people don't die from not having access to medical

Publishers, 2001.

[93] Breggin, Peter, *Psychiatry and the Holocaust—The Violence Initiative—Part 1*, YouTube video, 2010 upload, http://youtu.be/MQZdUmxG1Es

"care"—they die from the life constraints and liabilities directly resulting from poverty. How many MDs have stated this obvious truth on the radio?

Environmental Science Lies

Exploitation via resource extraction, land use expropriation, and wage slavery creation and maintenance are devastating to indigenous populations and to the environment on continental scales. It is therefore vital to cover up the crimes under a veil of expert analysis and policy development diversion. A valued class of service intellectuals here is composed of the environmental scientists and consultants.

Environmental scientists naively and knowingly work hand in hand with finance-corporate shysters, mainstream media, politicians, and state and international bureaucrats to mask real problems and to create profit opportunities for select power elites. Here are notable examples of specific cases.

Freon and Ozone

Do you know of anyone who has been killed by the ozone hole?

The 1987 Montreal Protocol banning chlorofluorocarbons (CFCs) is considered a textbook case where science and responsible governance lead to a landmark treaty for the benefit of the Earth and all its inhabitants. How often does that happen?

At about the time that the DuPont patent on Freon™, the most widely used CFC refrigerant in the world, was expiring the mainstream media picked up on otherwise arcane scientific observations and hypotheses about ozone concentration in the upper atmosphere near the poles.

There resulted an international mobilization to criminalize CFCs and DuPont developed and patented a replacement refrigerant that was promptly certified for use.

A Nobel Prize in chemistry was awarded in 1995 for a laboratory demonstration that CFCs could deplete ozone in simulated

Denis G. Rancourt

atmospheric conditions. In 2007 it was shown that the latter work may have been seriously flawed by overestimating the depletion rate by an order of magnitude, thereby invalidating the proposed mechanism for CFC-driven ozone depletion[94]. Not to mention that any laboratory experiment is somewhat different from the actual upper atmosphere...is the Nobel tainted by media and special interest lobbying?

It gets better. It turns out that the DuPont replacement refrigerant is, not surprisingly, not as inert as was Freon. As a result it corrodes refrigerator cycle components at a much faster rate. Where home refrigerators and freezers lasted forever, they now burn out in eight years or so. This has caused catastrophic increases in major appliance contributions to land fill sites across North America[95]; spurred on by the green propaganda for obscenely efficient electrical consumptions of the new appliances under closed door (zero use) conditions.

In addition, we have been frenzied into avoiding the sun, the UV index keeps our fear of cancer and our dependence on the medical establishment alive, and a new sun block industry a la vampire protection league has been spawned. And of course star university chemists are looking for that perfect sun block molecule that can be

---

[94] *Chemists poke holes in ozone theory: Reaction data of crucial chloride compounds called into question.* Nature 449, 382-383 (2007). http://www.nature.com/news/2007/070924/full/449382a.html

[95] With approximately 120 million households in the U.S., a refrigerator's life expectancy determines how many refrigerators go into landfills per year. With a present industry life expectancy of 14 years, the number is over 8 million refrigerators per year, not counting freezers and second refrigerators. Therefore, breakdowns due to internal corrosion are a critical factor, yet have not been duly studied or reported. Home safety and toxicity appear to be a few of the only approved concerns: Calm, J.M., *Refrigerant Safety*, ASHRAE Journal, vol.36, 1994, p.17-26; and see the EPA's *Questions and answers on alternative refrigerants*, http://www.epa.gov/ozone/snap/refrigerants/qa.html

113

patented by big pharma. And as soon as it is, I predict a surge in media interviews with skin cancer experts....

Acid Rain on the Boreal Forest

In the seventies it was acid rain. Thousands of scientists from around the world (Northern Hemisphere) studied this "most pressing environmental problem on the planet". The boreal forest is the largest ecosystem on Earth and its millions of lakes were reportedly being killed by acid from the sky.

Coal burning plants spewed out sulphides into the atmosphere causing the rain to be acidic. The acid rain was postulated to acidify the soils and lakes in the boreal forest but the acidification was virtually impossible to detect. Pristine lakes in the hearts of national parks had to be studied for decades in attempts to detect a statistically significant acidification.

Meanwhile the lakes and their watersheds were being destroyed by the cottage industry, agriculture, forestry, mining, over fishing and tourism. None of the local and regional destruction was studied or exposed. Instead, scientists turned their gaze to distant coal burning plants, atmospheric distribution, and postulated chemical reactions occurring in rain droplets. One study found that the spawning in aquarium of one fish species was extremely sensitive to acidity (pH). Long treatises about cation charge balance and transport were written and attention was diverted away from the destruction on the ground towards a sanitized problem of atmospheric chemistry that was the result of industrialization and progress rather than being caused by identifiable exploiters.

As a physicist and Earth scientist turned environmental scientist, I personally read virtually every single scientific paper written about acid rain and could not find an example of a demonstrated negative impact on lakes or forests from acid rain. In my opinion, contrary to the repeated claims of the scientist authors, the research on acid rain demonstrates that acid rain could not possibly have been the problem.

This model of elite-forces-coordinated exploiter whitewashing was to play itself out on an even grander scale only decades later with global warming.

Global Warming as a Threat to Humankind

In 2005 and 2006, several years before the November 2009 Climategate scandal burst the media bubble that buoyed public opinion towards acceptance of carbon credits, cap and trade, and the associated trillion dollar finance bonanza that may still come to pass, I exposed the global warming cooptation scam in an essay that Alexander Cockburn writing in The Nation[96] called "one of the best essays on greenhouse myth-making from a left perspective." [97] [98] [99].

My essay prompted David F. Noble to research the question and write *The Corporate Climate Coup* to expose how the media embrace followed the finance sector's realization of the unprecedented potential for revenues that going green could represent.[100]

Introductory paragraphs from *Global Warming: Truth or Dare?* are as follows:

> *I also advance that there are strong societal, institutional, and psychological motivations for having constructed and for continuing to maintain the myth of a global warming dominant threat*

---

[96] http://www.counterpunch.org/2007/06/09/dissidents-against-dogma/
[97] *Global Warming: Truth or Dare?*, Denis G. Rancourt, 2007. http://activistteacher.blogspot.ca/2007/02/global-warming-truth-or-dare.html
[98] *Questioning Climate Politics—Denis Rancourt says the 'global warming myth' is part of the problem*, April 11, 2007, interview in *The Dominion*. http://www.dominionpaper.ca/articles/1110
[99] Climate Guy blog. http://climateguy.blogspot.ca/
[100] *The Corporate Climate Coup*, David F. Noble, 2007. http://activistteacher.blogspot.ca/2007/05/dgr-in-my-article-entitled-global.html

> *(global warming myth, for short). I describe these motivations in terms of the workings of the scientific profession and of the global corporate and finance network and its government shadows.*
>
> *I argue that by far the most destructive force on the planet is power-driven financiers and profit-driven corporations and their cartels backed by military might; and that the global warming myth is a red herring that contributes to hiding this truth. In my opinion, activists who, using any justification, feed the global warming myth have effectively been co-opted, or at best neutralized.*

Other passages read this way:

> *Environmental scientists and government agencies get funding to study and monitor problems that do not threaten corporate and financial interests. It is therefore no surprise that they would attack continental-scale devastation from resource extraction via the CO_2 back door. The main drawback with this strategy is that you cannot control a hungry monster by asking it not to shit as much.*
>
> *Global warming is strictly an imaginary problem of the First World middleclass. Nobody else cares about global warming. Exploited factory workers in the Third World don't care about global warming. Depleted uranium genetically mutilated children in Iraq don't care about global warming. Devastated aboriginal populations the world over also can't relate to global warming, except maybe as representing the only solidarity that we might volunteer.*
>
> *It's not about limited resources. ["The amount of*

> *money spent on pet food in the US and Europe each*
> *year equals the additional amount needed to provide*
> *basic food and health care for all the people in poor*
> *countries, with a sizeable amount left over." (UN*
> *Human Development Report, 1999)] It's about*
> *exploitation, oppression, racism, power, and greed.*
> *Economic, human, and animal justice brings*
> *economic sustainability which in turn is always based*
> *on renewable practices. Recognizing the basic rights*
> *of native people automatically moderates resource*
> *extraction and preserves natural habitats. Not*
> *permitting imperialist wars and interventions*
> *automatically quenches nation-scale exploitation.*
> *True democratic control over monetary policy goes a*
> *long way in removing debt-based extortion. Etc.*

And there is a thorough critique of the science as band wagon trumpeting and interested self-deception. Climategate only confirms what should be obvious to any practicing scientist: That science is a mafia when it's not simply a sleeping pill.

Pure Madness

It just goes on and on. What is not a lie?

Look at the recent H1N1 scam—another textbook example. It's farcical how far these circuses go: antiseptic gels in every doorway at the blink of an eye; high school students getting high from drinking the alcohol in the gels; outdatedness of the viral strain before the pre-paid vaccine can be mass produced; unproven effectiveness; no requirement to prove effectiveness; government guarantees to corporate manufacturers against client lawsuits; university safety officers teaching students how to cough; etc.

Pure madness. Has something triggered our genetically ingrained First World stupidity reflex? Is this part of our march towards fascism?[101]

Here is another one. Educators promote the lie that we learn because we are taught. This lie of education is squarely denounced by radical educators.[102] [103]

University professors design curricula as though the students actually learn every element that is delivered whereas the truth is that students don't learn the delivered material and everyone only learns what they learn. One could dramatically change the order in which courses are delivered and it would make no measurable difference in how much students learn. Students deliver nonsense and professors don't care. Obedience and indoctrination are all that matter so the only required skill is bluffing. Students know this and those that don't don't know what they know, don't know themselves.

Pick any expert opinion or dominant paradigm: it's part of a racket. We can't know the truth because the truth is brutal.

Two (more recent) articles of note on the global warming front are my broad critique of the main science aspects[104] and my report on the physics of planetary radiation balance.[105] The latter free-access scientific article has been downloaded more than 800 times.

Despite the above dramatic examples of the extent and depth of the "web of lies" that fill our schools and mass media, it would be a mistake to think that population control in an "advanced" society can

---

[101] *Canadian Education as an Impetus towards Fascism*, Denis G. Rancourt, 2009. http://activistteacher.blogspot.ca/2010/01/canadian-education-as-impetus-towards.html

[102] *Pedagogy of the Oppressed*, Paulo Freire, 1970.

[103] *The Ignorant Schoolmaster*, Jacques Rancière, 1991.

[104] *On the gargantuan lie of climate change science*, Activist Teacher, March 21, 2011. http://activistteacher.blogspot.ca/2011/03/on-gargantuan-lie-of-climate-change.html

[105] *Radiation physics constraints on global warming: CO_2 increase has little effect*, on archive.org, December 3, 2011.
http://archive.org/details/RadiationPhysicsConstraintsOnGlobalWarmingCo2IncreaseHasLittleEffect

be achieved simply by creating and maintaining this mental environment of deceit. An additional crucial element is needed, without which the web of lies would not stick. The processes of perception and of critical assessment themselves must be altered so that the subjects can receive these vast fabrications as plausible truths.

The main moderator of perception is the hierarchy itself. Most individuals who buy-in derive their identities largely from their positions within the hierarchy. Here self-interest, in terms of preserving one's self-image or identity, is the dominant factor in turn determining perception and/or interpretation of the world. Nothing could be more true, in my opinion, regarding perception of social phenomena: we cannot perceive what would harm our self-image and we interpret the world to preserve an internal logic consistent with our identities. "Information gathering" is never objective but rather is a political activity of self-preservation.

For less integrated individuals, there is more risk of perceptions that are closer to the truth about the world. At the bottom, severe physical oppression solves this problem and keeps workers in line and undesirables excluded, segregated, or exterminated. This works as long as you can keep the workers or prisoners fighting each other and as long as you can keep them from talking to each other or interacting in any significant way that would allow growth. Incapacitating drugs as escapes, under-feeding, competition for food or privileges, elusive promises of liberation as leverage—it all works.

For the middle-ground less integrated individuals who are retained as functional at "higher" level, they must be made and kept stupid. They must be prevented from developing a capacity to understand the world, their place in the world, and themselves. Beyond the strict confines of institutional education, this is where anti-racism, like all systems of behavioural control aimed at inner thoughts and attitudes, plays a major role, which is the subject of the next chapter.

Beyond Disoriented, the Individual Must Be Incapacitated

HOW DID THE great North American revolutionaries of social change such as Mary Harris "Mother" Jones and Malcolm X get so smart and why were they not afraid of words and opinions?

The short answer is: conflict. They engaged. They advanced their ideas, as calls for self-defence and revolutionary action. As unpopular, sexist, and racist as were those ideas, they were what were needed to catalyze a strong resistance and awakening. Their campaigns called on their peoples to find the dignity to defend themselves, to stand and fight back.

They came, through struggle, to understand that there are only two options: you either oppose and resist or you cooperate with the system and integrate; that every choice of social participation is between these two positions. They came to believe that struggle was a needed equalizer and that, in the face of an unrelenting oppressor, dignity and meaning could only come from struggle against the oppressor.

They wanted a fair fight without the trappings of the collaborator's sophistry or the boss's imposed rules of constrained expression. Mother Jones denounced smooth talking collaborating union leaders every chance she had and Malcolm X both explained the meaning of "house negro" and called on whites to express their racism freely, as a starting point to engage in real dialogue.

As noted in the Overview, Malcolm X put it this way:

> *The only way the problem can be solved—first, the white man and the black man have to be able to sit down at the same table. The white man has to feel free to speak his mind without hurting the feelings of that Negro, and the so-called Negro has to feel free to speak his mind without hurting the feelings of the white man. Then they can bring the issues that are under the rug out on top of the table and take an intelligent approach to get the problem solved.*

If the established order imposes a regime of language correctness then there are two impacts on the individual. First, the individual must repress and internalize his or her reactions and interpretations rather than express them freely. Surviving Catholics[106] will recognize the "wisdom" of such a strategy. Second, the individual is deprived of hearing the free and authentic reactions of others and thereby deprived of intense occasions to challenge the other and to be challenged.

True, no two individuals have equal power and influence within a group. True there are race and gender and size and age biases. So what? No one is armed and power and influence are temporal attributes that one develops by engaging.

Use what you must to make your space but don't call on the hierarchical structure of dominance to regulate attitudes and

---

[106] By "surviving Catholic", I mean an individual who was first indoctrinated into the organized orthodoxy of Catholicism and later escaped via personal rebellion and liberation. Organized Catholicism has formalized and perfected the art of the internalized oppressor to extremes of self-guilt and self-consciousness, as is well known in popular culture.

expression at the broadest possible scales. That is pure poison.

Otherwise, individuals are kept in a sterile environment in which they are deprived of much needed conflict, the interactional conflict that would help them discover themselves and others, and that would generate growth, discernment, definition, and self-confidence.

This is a main deleterious effect of anti-racism, as a lobbying, policy, and educational project. It eliminates needed inter-personal interactions within horizontal strata of the dominance hierarchy, while maintaining inter-strata racism. Eliminating "strife" and "violence" in this way, as a top-down social engineering exercise, contributes to atomizing individuals, not by physical separation but by disallowing intense inter-personal interactions.

Those who advocate anti-racism generally seek to both integrate and to derive status and influence in their roles advocating this social engineering project, or are simply drawn by the promise of paternalistic protection in the guise of a beneficial public policy umbrella. The oft heard immature refrain is: I should not have to suffer the constant burden of struggle just to get my due.

Individuals have natural abilities to fight their own battles. State-imposed "non-violence" rules regarding inter-personal interactions stunt the development of those abilities and generate a reliance on the state to moderate human relations. By any measure and according to many studies, the state is a disastrous parent. Why would we ask it to keep us separated and stunted in this way?

No anti-bullying or anti-mobbing policy can ever be effective without victims willing to defend themselves. And the best self-defence training ground is one where authentic discourse is allowed and is moderated by inter-personal reactions rather than dominance-structure-imposed guilt-trips and state-imposed legal sanctions. Societies of expressive individuals are healthy societies.

The starting point must be who we are. Not a policy directive. In interaction we develop and make culture and politics. Under policy we are maintained and impoverished.

Denis G. Rancourt

An effective anti-racism policy that we adopt serves to moderate our interactions via self-censorship, depriving us of interactional conflict. It thereby bars us from discovering our power and influence in struggle and hides reality from us, the reality of others and the truth that change comes from struggle, not policy.

We never learn the lesson but instead learn to have faith in policy, policy that never quite solves racism....

Anti-Racism as an Instrument of Hierarchical Power

LET ME START this chapter by boldly making the following anarchic/libertarian pronouncement about the value of free speech in combating illegitimate control structures: individual free expression of racist opinions is only harmful in an oppressive hierarchical environment where structural racism exists and where psychological mobbing mechanisms can spontaneously develop. The best antidote to both is to allow and encourage individual free expression so that racism can be exposed and challenged along with the oppressive overriding power structures.

To participate in the suppression of any individual expression, including an expression correctly characterized as an individual's "hate speech," is to violate the individual's right to free expression. Such systemic discriminatory suppression is a sign of societal feebleness[107] where paternalistic control is sought as protection in lieu of independent thought. To insist on such state "protection" is to

---

[107] By "societal feebleness" I mean a society in which the majority of individuals are weak, underdeveloped, and unhealthy. Strong dominance hierarchies, tending towards corporate fascism and totalitarianism, engender feeble societies, including the individuals of the masses oppressed by the said hierarchy.

assume the victim stance for some and for others it is to refuse the personal day-to-day political responsibility to stand for the rights of all individuals. It is to legitimize the state in violating individual freedom.

The latter is not a popular stance in the "progressive" left. We have come to a point where freedom of expression is routinely vilified as a pretext to practice racism and where any resistance to anti-racism policies is itself considered racism. Many "progressives" candidly admit that they support anti-racist censorship "for the good of the community."

We live in an era where given the Nazi holocaust, one cannot be critical of the state of Israel without being accused of anti-Semitism, and given the murderous racism of the Ku Klux Klan, one cannot be critical of anti-racism policies or laws without being accused of at least latent racism. We also live an era of such self-consciousness and good will (or propensity for mobbing as a legitimate means of societal influence?) that these accusations of anti-Semitism and latent racism carry a lot of weight.

From my tentative anarchic/libertarian perspective, therefore, I next address the apparent systemic purpose of anti-racism policy, as ascertained from its actual impacts. Here are three essays that explore this question.

Critical Race Theory, in the Service of Whitey[108]

Take the most "progressive" recent development in social design theory in the First World. Take critical race theory, as developed in the seminal essays collected in the 1993 book *Words That Wound: Critical Race Theory, Assaultive Speech, and the First Amendment*, by legal scholars Mari Matsuda, Charles Lawrence III, Richard Delgado, and Kimberlè Crenshaw.

Critical race theory is the accepted justificative framework for

---

[108] This essay was first published on the *Activist Teacher* blog, August 2011.

hate speech laws, codes and policies. As a discipline, it has exerted significant impact in the academic areas of feminism, race studies, pedagogy, and the social sciences in general.

But is critical race theory soundly based as an interpretive scheme that is likely to produce more justice in society or is it a lie?

Critical race theory operates on two social design fronts:

(1)   to aid us all in our analysis, detection and deconstruction of Eurocentric views, interpretations, and systems; and

(2)   to motivate development and implementation of hate speech laws and "hurtful or assaultive language" codes and policies, aimed at moving spoken language away from all isms (racism, classism, sexism, etc.).

The underlying assumed social change model in which critical race theory operates is one where having institutionalized or sectarian (such as peer-group-driven) and enforceable rules of language behaviour make both society and individuals healthier.

Second-tier underlying assumptions include: (a) that the isms are intrinsically bad, lead to worse things (such as war and genocide) and should be removed, and (b) that rules and social engineering in general (education, marketing, laws and rules, etc.) help to remove the isms and are an effective method for doing so.

Some of the above assumptions and their legal consequences have been elucidated and brilliantly critiqued in the context of historical case law and jurisprudence by the renowned scholar Henry Louis Gates Jr. (who, critical race theory enthusiasts will be interested to know, is black) in his 1996 essay *Critical Race Theory and Freedom of Speech*[109].

---

[109] Gates, Henry Jouis Jr., *Critical Race Theory and Freedom of Speech*, Chapter Five in "The Future of Academic Freedom", Menard, Louis, Ed., University of Chicago Press, 1996.

That critical race theory is potentially a lie can be ascertained by a quick reference to the anarchist model of spontaneous social change and maintenance, arguably the most powerful model of primal social tensions.

Anarchy theory posits the rarely contested view that individual behaviour is primarily determined by norms and values transmitted by the individual's community which in turn is shaped by the individual. Only imposed atomization and a strong external dominance hierarchy (external to the individual's true community which he/she influences) can deteriorate the natural community-based determinations of individual behaviour.

The anarchist interpretation is that the legal system and all rules imposed on all are integral parts of an oppressive dominance hierarchy. Add to this the scientific result that dominance hierarchy is by far the major cause of health problems and death of individuals and one must wonder how more laws, relating to entirely new crimes and that directly impinge on individual freedoms, could make society better.

Unless one accepts the absurd proposition that uttered words should in themselves be considered assaults (punishable by institutions) irrespective of context and intent, or the equally absurd notion that intent is irrelevant and the only relevant context is the skin colour (or sex or class, etc.) of the person who hears the uttered words, then we must admit that critical race theory concerns itself with thought crimes and attitude crimes.

This brings us to seek some truth regarding how thoughts and attitudes of individuals are best developed and changed, best in the sense of health and emancipation not in the sense of imposed productivity or expected apparent civility.

The idiocy of expecting to steer social development via fine-tuned laws and "good" rulings is up there with the idiocy of expecting that learning is optimized by designing the ideal curriculum. These are the operational lies (and the deceitful masks) of jurisprudence and education, respectively.

Emotional hurt within a class stratum of the dominance hierarchy (distinct from stress from the oppression delivered by the dominance hierarchy) is a metabolic reaction of the individual. It belongs to and informs the individual. It cannot be the basis for quantifying harm done by someone else, in view of a systemic punishment. To move in the latter direction is to move closer to a particularly sick hierarchal society.

The individual can use the information of his/her metabolic reaction of hurt emotions in a personal decision-making process and choose to intervene within the hierarchical stratum to request adjustments of others in his/her community. There the negotiation of personal relationships starts. This intervention can include any of the pressure mechanisms that individuals possess to influence other individuals, and it is always mediated by community.

It is this process of expressed conflicting perspectives, of political leveraging within the community, of vehement disagreements, and of everything that it is to establish one's place and to influence community that is vital. This process should not be constrained from outside or follow any dogma or behavioural prescription. The only valid guiding principle is that it should be authentic and free, whether judged hurtful or not. It is this individual freedom of communicative interaction, unavoidably and naturally mediated by community, which produces both growth of the individual and development of the community.

This collective discourse is especially needed in diverse communities and is needed as an integral part of the praxis of liberation from oppression. Any constraints from hierarchical rules and dogmatic behavioural prescriptions can only frustrate change and oppress individuals.

Sure, choose your friends and create safe spaces but don't go around prescribing general thought, attitude and behavioural rules anchored in the dominance hierarchy. And don't expect society itself to become or be made a "safe space" by passing laws and rules. The only way to contribute to bettering society is to directly fight one's own oppression, with the measured risks that this entails. This is so obvious that it needs to be stated.

In fact, most of us are blind to the obvious because we have allowed ourselves to be defined by the dominance hierarchy. Within this definition, we have no power or influence except through the structures of the hierarchy. But all of these structures can at best only make the slavery more just, as we vie to be fairly oppressed.

The critical race theorists of the legal profession are new-wave law theorists looking to lead a legal analysis sect premised on continued slave-hood and the law as protective master and paternalistic guardian of society's values.

In a world where all the resources are controlled undemocratically and wealth and power are hyper-concentrated, in a world where the latter is legal and exploitation is legally protected by force, hate speech laws against ordinary individuals are a profound absurdity, as are defamation laws applicable against ordinary individuals. As long as the law is power-biased and hierarchy-preserving, it is against people. Systems perpetrate war and genocide irrespective of what powerless individuals say, especially if individual expression is curtailed.

Critical race theory is a lie—another one that serves whitey.

How Anti-Racism Protects Class Structure and Dominance Hierarchy[110]

I consider that there is a fundamental distinction to be made between (1) racism of belief or opinion of the individual and (2) racism of action (or inaction) in the systemic oppression of others.

There is an extensive and baseless sociological literature advancing that belief or opinion racism of the individual (on its own and largely independent of the hierarchical context) generates racist

---

[110] This essay was first published on *Activist Teacher*, April 2011.

oppressions of peoples, all the way to genocide.

The latter proposal is used to advance the "obvious solution" that belief or opinion racism of the individual must be continuously eradicated using coercive methods including: propaganda, "education", the legal apparatus, and the state-NGO-civil-society anti-oppression complex.

In other words, the physical reality of dominance hierarchy oppression racism is supposedly "attacked at its root" by social engineering premised on attitude manipulation of the individual— who is treated as being infected with racism in the same way that one would have a malignant tumour that can be surgically removed.

Agency and responsibility are turned away from attacking the racist dominance structure directly; by focusing on a false and ancillary "cause", by blaming the internal beliefs of some individuals instead of emphasizing the needed praxis of liberation of all individuals subjected to the dominance hierarchy.

What results is a classic divide and conquer strategy where oppressed victims are divided by race, gender, etc., and where a hierarchy of the oppressions becomes the focus within each stratum of the dominance hierarchy instead of actual fighting back.

What results is that the slaves fight among themselves to ensure that they are oppressed fairly. There is a focus on defining and enforcing inter-slave rules instead of supporting rebellion.

What results is that each group in the hierarchy of the oppressions is further cantonized and embedded into its victimhood while insisting that the solution is for the "less" (or not) oppressed individuals to "recognize their privilege" and to change their ingrained oppressive behaviours.

Following Freire, I believe that the latter approach is a senseless tactic and a harmful diversion[111]:

> [T]he oppressor, who is himself dehumanized because

---

[111] *Pedagogy of the Oppressed*, Paulo Freire, 1970.

> *he dehumanizes others, is unable to lead this*
> *struggle. However, the oppressed...are inhibited from*
> *waging the struggle for freedom so long as they feel*
> *incapable of running the risks it requires....*
>
> *It is only the oppressed who, by freeing*
> *themselves, can free their oppressors. The latter, as an*
> *oppressive class, can free neither others nor*
> *themselves....*

The problem with disallowing all violence is that it removes violence as a means for self-defence against a violent attacker. To disallow the use of force is to support the oppressor who uses force by unjustly depriving the oppressed of an important instrument of self-defence.[112]

Similarly, much oppression is race-based, where the oppressor class is racially defined. In such circumstances it is a natural defence mechanism for the oppressed to recognize the oppressor on a race basis. Here the oppressed need to be racist as a question of survival and efficient self-defence.

Indeed, it is a natural instinct to learn to recognize dangerous animal species or predatory groups of the same species. Such "racism" is an essential survival reflex. Such an ingrained reflex is practiced and modified by culture. It is part of our humanity. Like violence, it is not in itself and out of context positive or negative. Only the objective circumstances that make racism or violence necessary or advantageous as part of self-defence are objectively negative.

Therefore, to attack belief or opinion racism rather than the oppressors who have created the circumstances for the development

---

[112] *Pacifism as Pathology*, Ward Churchill, 1998; *How Nonviolence Protects The State*, Peter Gelderloos, 2007; *On the racism and pathology of left progressive First-World activism*, Denis G. Rancourt, 2010, http://activistteacher.blogspot.ca/2010/08/on-racism-and-pathology-of-left.html

of racism is to substitute one effect of the dominance hierarchy for the cause. As a consequence one mostly avoids the necessary (and feared) confrontation against the oppressor.

At a given time and place, whites are either in solidarity or are oppressors. If they are in solidarity then they also must fight the common oppressors. If they are oppressors then they must be fought. It is not an attitudes workshop. It is a praxis of liberation driven by authentic rebellion.

The anti-racism of thought crime racism is a barrier to free expression and to the dialectic interactions that must occur within one's stratum of the dominance hierarchy, within each community. As long as there is the possibility between individuals to challenge, insult, verbally intimidate, attempt to convince, reason, seduce, influence, shame, expose, and so on, without significant objective consequences to physical safety and well-being and without resorting to mobbing then the conditions exist to build community. As soon as one appeals to organized coercion, irrespective of the grand principle being espoused, then one is representing and supporting the hierarchical oppressor and generating a new intra-stratum control structure.

All structures that stabilize and reinforce slave relations while masking or impeding the possibility of rebellion support slavery.

An activism centered on creating a "safe space" by the method of internal organization rather than by pushing out the invader is an activism that supports that all other spaces are not safe. And its "safe spaces" will never be safe or even feel safe.

Community building must be an integral part of liberation. It cannot be an escape from the oppression of the dominance hierarchy. It cannot be an avoidance of liberation, no matter how sophisticated. An internalized and invisible oppression is the most devastating.

Denis G. Rancourt

Anti-Racist and Anti-Violence Proscriptions Enable Oppression[113]

Violence itself is neither good nor bad. The persistent and widespread crimes of war, population-displacement, genocide, slavery, and economic exploitation thrive on a vile violence of the powerful who occupy, oppress and suppress those made-vulnerable. But the needed violence of the victims for self-defence is noble. One violence is vile, the other is noble.

To prescribe sweeping pacifism is both to enable the crimes of violence of the powerful and to deny the rights of their victims, indeed to deny the humanity of the victims.[114] [115] [116] Pacifism proscriptions aimed at obedient workers and consumers (not police and soldiers) are continuously echoed by the pronouncements of power's service intellectuals and image managers.

How does the nonsense of doctrinal non-violence masquerading as a theory of "social change" arise and why does it persist, in the face of all evidence?

Dichotomous categorization is a strong intrinsic tendency of the human brain, anchored in the hard-wired binary fight or flight survival decision mechanism. As a result, in constructing the social self-talk of helpful recipes for our everyday lives we automatically and falsely "identify" binary good-bad pairs and categorize a given emotion or action or reaction as either good or bad in its own right rather than seek a deeper analysis of the broader circumstances

---

[113] This essay was first published on the *Activist Teacher* blog, December 2011.

[114] *Pacifism as pathology*, Ward Churchill, 1998.

[115] *Pedagogy of the oppressed*, Paulo Freire, 1970.

[116] *On the racism and pathology of left progressive First-World activism*, Denis G. Rancourt, 2010.
http://activistteacher.blogspot.com/2010/08/on-racism-and-pathology-of-left.html

determined by an array of factors. Since the individual's role is delimited by hierarchy a deep individual analysis is a threat to the individual's status within the hierarchy.

We thus arrive at nonsensical superficial conclusions such as that there are "negative" and "positive" emotions that in themselves need to be sought or avoided rather than objectively viewing emotions as metabolic messengers for acting in the world. This is a modern symptom of our detachment from community and from ourselves; a detachment driven by the dominance hierarchy that controls our lives.

In this way, violence and racism are superficially categorized as both negative and to be avoided in themselves and are outlawed in society—rather than attempting to ascertain the circumstances of the particular violence or racism that may make the violence or racism both sane and beneficial.

Racism itself is neither good nor bad. The racism of the oppressor facilitates violent oppression. But the racism of the oppressed is part of a communal mechanism of self-defence.

For example, it is natural and efficacious self-defence for an occupied or oppressed group to be racist against the occupier or oppressor. Minority Chinese immigrants are *a priori* justified in shielding their children from marriages with "white devils". A culture supporting global carnage and colonization is one to be avoided. It is judicious for a minority group in a Western country to viscerally associate white skin with danger that is to be avoided.

There is a strong and natural human affinity to racism, informed by millions of years of animal evolution. A vulnerable species needs to recognize predators and associate key predator characteristics with danger and repulsion. Sedentary or nomadic tribes need to recognize more aggressive predatory groups by whatever racial or other characteristics are available. And so on, as a matter of self-defence. And, when it comes to invaders who rape, pillage and kidnap, it serves to preserve a strong and durable cultural memory via racism embedded in individual psychology.

Denis G. Rancourt

Liberal sweeping anti-racism proscriptions are an immature attempt to deny reality; anchored in the false belief that behavioural dictates determine societal truths. The accompanying liberal policies, laws, etc., are a how-to guide for sticking one's head in the sand. Is there less sexual perversion among those who practice polite discourse? Is a Canadian mining corporation operating in Latin America or the Congo less racist because of its anti-racist employment practices at home office? Or more environmental because the home office recycles? (Those who answered yes to the last few questions can stop reading at this point.)

Democratic liberal society's recent blanket anti-racism proscriptions managed by the service elites represent systemic attempts to counter the natural affinity for racism, and are structurally intended as an operational device to facilitate intra-species inter-race cooperation for assimilation in the modern urban corporate economy.

A sweeping anti-racism proscription facilitates economic exploitation in a unified workforce model and protects the bosses from being racially identified. Negating individual thought and opinion-racism serves to hide the economy's racism of dominance, and hierarchical dominance itself (we are all equal).

Anti-racism assimilation strengthens and feeds the dominant "culture" (elite groups) most tied to the invading hierarchy, a process known on the planetary scale as "globalization". Superpowers use racism to divide and conquer competing systems and "combat racism" in assimilating conquered peoples. (Federal "bilingualism" is used in a similar way to assimilate French Quebec into English Canada.)

Here, a broad anti-racism facade also facilitates the recruitment of large arrays of needed service leaders and managers of the same race(s) as the race(s) to be handled. It's easier for the home office to cleanse a territory of brown people on another continent if home office First World middle-class managers and press officers are multi-coloured.

Sweeping anti-racism in the form of behavioural proscriptions

135

within liberal so-called free and democratic (i.e., stable self-indoctrinated) societies actually helps to preserve the racism of the oppressors and inter-class racism.[117]

Racism cannot be eliminated, no more than "negative" emotions can be eliminated. Instead, racism must be identified and used within its true context of class struggle and anti-oppression self-defence. Down racism (directed down the hierarchy) must be continuously fought. Up racism (directed up the hierarchy) should be optimally applied while being vigilant to maintain its "up" orientation. Horizontal racism within a hierarchical stratum must be diffused and channelled into up racism or up classism.

In this way, by a continuous acknowledgement of racism, by a continuous discernment of the type of racism active in the context of fighting one's own oppression, and by recognizing that racism is unequally by-directional in hierarchical oppression, a realistically complex concept of racism emerges as a natural tool that helps one better perceive and gauge one's own oppression. The anti-oppression struggle, distinct from but intertwined with the struggle of community building, becomes primary and race becomes secondary. Inter-class racism is gone when one can use racial language in critiquing an inter-class member in the same way one would refer to any other personal characteristic, without prejudice.

Inter-class racism used to leverage inter-class advantage or hierarchical "advancement" is a crass form of opportunism. It is a modern derivative racism, a device sustained by "free and democratic" hierarchical systems, not primitively related to survival and oppression racisms.

The Right feels disdain for any sign of formalized leverage racism at a gut instinct level as it clings to its myth of a level playing

---

[117] *How anti-racism protects class structure and dominance hierarchy*, Denis G. Rancourt, 2011.
http://activistteacher.blogspot.com/2011/04/how-anti-racism-protects-class.html

field (fair competition) supervised by responsible parents (institutional or natural-rules or invisible hand).

The Left wants to be managed (oppressed) fairly as it clings to its own myth of just and beneficial social engineering (elite manipulation).

Non-aligned individuals, independent thinkers and agents, need to responsibly accept and deal with the realities of violence and racism. "No war but the class war!"[118]

---

[118] Libertarian anti-militarism slogan. For an analysis of the role of class in war see: Parenti, Michael, *Blackshirts and Reds: Rational Fascism and the Overthrow of Communism*, 1997, City Lights Books. Parenti derides what he calls "ABC theorists", Anything But Class.

On the Specific Meaning of the Term "house negro" and On Its Tactical Use[119]

EVERY REVOLUTION HAS a counter-revolution. The establishment provides continuous resources to eliminate resistance. Justice-minded independent thinkers navigate a sea of deception. Powerful words are constantly transformed into non-threatening phrases geared towards creating compliance and self-monitoring.

A brilliant liberation strategist finds just the right language and collaborating service intellectuals are on it. They will first try to bar its use as being "excessive," "confrontational" (used as a negative), and "counter-productive." If this assault is not successful, then they will, in the longer run, "create the needed interpretive framework".

A prominent example is Malcolm X's "house negro" term for modern use.[120] What could be clearer in terms of identifying disguised collaborators against Black liberation? One solution is to make the term itself into a "racist slur", thereby putting everyone on

---

[119] A short version of this essay was first posted on the *Activist Teacher* blog, March, 2012.

[120] I use lower case first letters on both "house" and "negro" in the term "house negro" to emphasize the term as an inseparable whole expression, which has been adapted to non-Black contexts, rather than stress "Negro" as though one were simply characterizing members of the Negro race.

guard against its use.

Another avenue is to dilute its meaning and to apply it only selectively against the highest profile Black public figures such as Barack Obama and Condoleezza Rice, rather than in the daily local resistance struggle.

This essay is a call to be clear on the modern meaning of the term "house negro".

Arguably the first definition of "service intellectual" was given in my 2006 essay "Gradual change is not progress" [121]:

> *Comfortable First World liberal and left intellectuals claiming to work for change often project the opinion that positive change is best achieved by incremental improvements, gradual progress, dialogue, and negotiations that acknowledge the legitimacy of the other side. They assert that confrontation is 'counter productive'. There is an army of academics, managers, and professionals, who will argue this point quite strenuously. They are the service intellectuals.*
>
> *Their job is to block any model that would involve people of the disadvantaged side actually demanding change in the structure that keeps them at the bottom. Instead, they promote a dialogue model in which the disadvantaged side enters into loaded and unwinnable negotiations with players that hold all the cards. These negotiations ensure that institutional structures of inequity are reinforced rather than progressively dismantled. [...]*

---

[121] *Gradual change is not progress*, Denis G. Rancourt, Global Research, May 3, 2006.
http://www.globalresearch.ca/index.php?context=viewArticle&code=R AN20060503&articleId=2377

In retrospect, the term is a race-neutral version of the "house negro" term defined for modern use by Malcolm X.[122] It is race-neutral in the sense that service intellectuals are recruited, for superior benefits and specialized service, irrespective of race: any advantageous personal characteristic will do.

Both these terms, "service intellectual" and "house negro", are precise, needed, and powerful in liberation praxis. And it is important to preserve their meanings without allowing dilution or imprecision or re-casting.

Therefore, I want to stress the difference between a "service intellectual" and what I will call a "service manager"; or between a "house negro" and what one could call a "manager negro".

Many critics will be outraged at my alleged disrespect as a white man to be defining terms such as "house negro" and "manager negro" and would have me chastised, fired, sued, or jailed. To you I say four things:

1. Good sense is where you find it.
2. Would you prefer that a service intellectual—of any colour—define the terms?
3. Most whites when they talk about race say shit but a white can be right on race.
4. Suppression of freedom of expression is harmful.

Unlike a "service intellectual" ("house negro"), a "service manager" ("manager negro") is not primarily concerned with image and mental environment maintenance but instead has the primary assigned task of managing some sector or enterprise for the hierarchical bosses.

In a "race conscious" racialized hierarchy of dominance it is useful for white masters to employ black managers. But it is more

---

[122] *The autobiography of Malcolm X*, told by Alex Haley, Random House, 1964; Chapter 14. http://autobiography-of-malcolm-x.wikispaces.com/14_black_muslims

than useful in terms only of "race relations" it is also simple recruitment from the appropriate class base and it can be strategic in terms of the sector or enterprise to be managed.

Given these distinctions, I would say that figures such as U.S. president Obama are more "manager negroes" than they are "house negroes"; just as the modern white presidents were mostly manager whiteys rather than service intellectuals (no argument there!). To call Obama a "house negro" is to dilute and weaken the term. He is primarily a manager.

I suggest we preserve the meaning intended by Malcolm X, following his years of study in a unique prison library and years of battle in the public arena and avoid most of the newer "hogwash" meanings proposed by the ever growing army of service intellectuals and manager academics. [123] [124] As stated by Malcolm X (Autobiography, Chapter 14):

> *Since slavery, the American white man has always kept some handpicked Negroes who fared much better than the black masses suffering and slaving out in the hot fields. The white man had these "house" and "yard" Negroes for his special servants. He threw them more crumbs from his rich table, he even let them eat in his kitchen. He knew that he could always count on them to keep "good massa" happy in his self-image of being so "good" and "righteous." "Good massa" always heard just what he wanted to hear from these "house" and "yard" blacks. "You're such a good, fine*

---

[123] [3] *Critical race theory, in the service of whitey*, Denis G. Rancourt, Activist Teacher blog, 2011.
http://activistteacher.blogspot.ca/2011/08/critical-race-theory-in-service-of.html
[124] [4] *'Anti-racism' in support of racism*, Denis G. Rancourt, Activist Teacher blog, 2011. http://activistteacher.blogspot.ca/2011/10/anti-racism-in-support-of-racism.html

massa!" Or, "Oh, massa, those old black nigger fieldhands out there, they're happy just like they are; why, massa, they're not intelligent enough for you to try and do any better for them, massa—

Well, slavery time's "house" and "yard" Negroes had become more sophisticated, that was all. When now the white man picked up his telephone and dialed his "house" and "yard" Negroes—why, he didn't even need to instruct the trained black puppets. They had seen the television program; had read the newspapers. They were already composing their lines. They knew what to do.

I'm not going to call any names. But if you make a list of the biggest Negro "leaders," so-called, in 1960, then you've named the ones who began to attack us "field" Negroes who were sounding insane, talking that way about "good massa."

By no means do these Muslims represent the Negro masses— That was the first worry, to reassure "good massa" that he had no reason to be concerned about his fieldhands in the ghettoes. "An irresponsible hate cult"..."an unfortunate Negro image, just when the racial picture is improving—"

In addition to diluting the term "house negro", the other counter-liberation tactic is to so vilify the term as to make it universally unacceptable, even among blacks. This is achieved in two steps. First, one postulates the usual "racism is bad" irrespective of context absolute. Second, one advances that certain words such as "negro", when used as part of a criticism, are intrinsically racist, that the term "house negro" is a racist slur. It follows that using the term "house negro" is racist, and therefore unacceptable in society.

Of course, the technical point that "racism" is *defined* as belief in intrinsic superiority (or inferiority) on the basis of race, and/or as discrimination on the basis of race, is not even a consideration when a service intellectual or the establishment so decides to canonize a term in itself as being a "racial slur", irrespective of intent or context, and irrespective of the political dimension.

Anti-liberation strategists typically go one step further to amplify the unacceptability of the term "house negro". They advance that to call a black person a house negro is to state that the said black person is a "race traitor", a pariah in "the Black community", and a person who has forfeited his/her racial identity. When status-disadvantaged blacks make these "race traitor" statements, they mean "you have betrayed us". But when those protecting the collaborators and the collaborators themselves make these same "race traitor" statements, they intend to amplify the insult received to an unacceptable level: "You accuse me, a black person who must carry my blackness wherever I go, of not being black!?"

In other words, the "race traitor" device, in the mouth of the establishment, is one where race is again used as an absolute in order to blur the fundamental class distinction which is inherent in the "house negro" term. In a hierarchical context, there is no "*the* Black community" because blacks are divided by class. The house negro chooses the side of house negroes and works against field negroes. The house negro protects the interests of black house negroes, and therefore the term "house negro" cannot also mean "race traitor" without accepting that field negroes are more representative of the Black race. Since the house negro does not accept the latter when he/she uses the "race traitor" device to cast the "house negro" term as an unacceptable supreme insult that cannot be uttered against a black person, then this device is logically invalid.

Muddled thinking on social issues comes from compliance, and is usually not thinking at all. Malcolm X's clear thinking about the "house negro" criticism came from his praxis. He provided an eminent historical example of the benefits of the use of the "house negro" criticism. Malcolm X explained how and why, in his view,

Martin Luther King was an Uncle Tom, in part:[125]

> *The white man pays Reverend Martin Luther King,*
> *subsidizes Reverend Martin Luther King, so that*
> *Reverend Martin Luther King can continue to teach*
> *the Negroes to be defenseless. That's what you mean*
> *by non-violent: be defenseless. Be defenseless in the*
> *face of one of the most cruel beasts that has ever*
> *taken a people into captivity. That's this American*
> *white man. And they have proved it throughout the*
> *country by the police dogs and the police clubs.*
>
> *A hundred years ago they used to put on a white*
> *sheet and use a bloodhound against Negroes. Today*
> *they've taken off the white sheet and put on police*
> *uniforms, they've traded in the bloodhounds for*
> *police dogs, and they're still doing the same thing.*
> *And just as Uncle Tom, back during slavery, used to*
> *keep the Negroes from resisting the bloodhound, or*
> *resisting the Ku Klux Klan, by teaching them to love*
> *their enemy, or pray for those who use them*
> *spitefully, today Martin Luther King is just a 20th*
> *century or modern Uncle Tom, or a religious Uncle*
> *Tom, who is doing the same thing today, to keep*
> *Negroes defenseless in the face of an attack, that*
> *Uncle Tom did on the plantation to keep those*
> *Negroes defenseless in the face of the attacks of the*
> *Klan in that day.*

Dr. King did not attack Malcolm X but rather became more radicalized in pursuing his work; as he went on to vehemently

---

[125] *Malcolm X: The White Man Pays Reverend Martin Luther King*, YouTube video of TV interview, http://youtu.be/nIdfVxCttZQ

denounce the Vietnam War[126]. King went on to position the civil rights movement against US warring, thereby additionally threatening both recruitment and acceptance of the war. Malcolm X's harsh and insulting criticism of Dr. King was part of needed interactions which enriched the broad movement of liberation.

---

[126] Martin Luther King, *Why I Am Opposed to the War in Vietnam*, YouTube video of sermon, Sermon at the Ebenezer Baptist Church on April 30, 1967. http://youtu.be/b80Bsw0UG-U

The Institutional and Hierarchical Context of Anti-Racism

SOME GENERAL RULES emerge from the above explorations. Chomsky has popularized the golden rule of institutions (or control structures) that a system will never do anything to harm itself. I propose further such rules that should inform our racism and societal analyses.

1. An institution will never do anything that would harm the institution.

2. An institution, beyond maintenance, always works to increase its power and control.

This arises from the bio-metabolic positive feedback mechanism for increased hierarchy explained above. A dominance hierarchy will always produce "runaway hierarchy" up to the point of resistance from individuals who, temporarily, can't be pushed any further, or up to a point of rebellion and revolutionary re-set. The institution constantly manipulates the physical and mental environments in order to always re-position the push-back point as far as possible towards increased hierarchy.

This rule overrides the naïve notion that capitalist institutions (or corporations) always maximize short-term financial profit. On the contrary, institutions readily sacrifice profit and productive competitiveness for more control over the workforce or a competitor.[127]

3. Any institution's outlay of resources is always aimed at maintaining and increasing the institution's power and control.

This rule suggests that since critical race theory is a product of universities, and since its regulatory product (codes of conduct, speech laws, etc.) is a product of the system, it was developed to address a system liability.

I have argued above that the system liability is that if individuals are allowed to have frank and unmonitored exchanges then this will give rise to strong emotional reactions, more and deeper exchanges, personal growth, and increased independence.

Any significant organized outlay of resources aimed at a specific alleged "improvement" (whether the effort is directed from the top or does not emanate from any single rigid command structure) is always actually aimed at a system liability—it always addresses some facet of a real or perceived or anticipated need of the system, in terms of maintaining and increasing its power and control.

The system does not allocate resources to make the lives of people better, only to strengthen and extend itself. In observing any outlay of effort, therefore, one can search for an underlying reason in terms of addressing some particular liability of the dominance hierarchy.

Another race example that should be analyzed is "affirmative

---

[127] Noble, David F., *Progress Without People*, Between The Lines, 1995; *Forces of Production: A Social History of Industrial Automation*, Oxford University Press, 1984.

action" or "equal opportunity employment". Not the idealistic variety proposed by well-meaning socialists and liberals, but the actual policies and their actual implementations. These programs also may be the product of the system addressing one of its liabilities, rather than primarily the outcome of grassroots activism, as follows.

The biggest problem with racism is state racism with its manifestations in terms of economic segregation, physical segregation (prisons, reserves), international exploitation, domestic exploitation, and war. These manifestations are so widespread and devastating, and the class divides are so imperfect, that there is some danger of intra-class concern and self-image angst in the middle, managerial, and professional classes.

Those elements of the middle, managerial, and professional classes that could be perturbed into resistance, given this disconnect between system values and local values polluted by inter-class contacts, need to be assimilated into contentedness. Therefore, racism must be masked in middle, managerial, and professional worker environments. Token visible minorities are needed and the risk of expressed racism of opinion must be minimized, as a demonstration that progress is being made or is sufficient and so that self-image can be salvaged.

In general, anti-racism has the utility that everyone "participates" in the "solution", both by adopting the model that racism can be fixed with policies about hiring and language rules and by "checking" oneself for one's attitudes and beliefs. In this way, racism is transformed from a problem of systemic oppression, suppression, and exploitation into a problem of individual self-improvement in interactions with one's colleagues.

No worries, the system can go on and that career promotion is still in the cards.

One should add that the institution's outlay of resources to maintain power and control is not simply an accounting of resources but it is generally also remarkably creative. The system discovers liabilities when individuals push back, and then adapts by a myriad of ways that include violent targeting and elimination, but also formal integration if the end result is greater institutional power and control. Since the individual's perception is predominantly determined by the individual's hierarchical status, it is not difficult for the hierarchy to deflect a criticism by feigning agreement via boldly redefining the words of the agreement, for "our own good" of course. As a result, the "agreement in principle" reached at the bargaining table is always in the final wording, which is the next real battle. Then, each subsequent tribunal or judicial ruling will re-define the words themselves, and on we go.

4. Every institution, as an instrument of a dominance hierarchy, is violently oppressive of the people who are its subjects.

Violence against the subject, as explained above in the words of Paulo Freire, is an inescapable consequence of the nature of hierarchy. The violence is palpable and evident, even in the professional work environment[128]:

> *[H]ierarchical power structures are inherently violent. The few can't maintain their authority over the many through rhetoric alone. Although bosses, for example, rarely use guards or police, their right to do so influences people's behavior, most obviously during individual confrontations and strikes. More importantly, on a daily basis, hierarchies subordinate and humiliate and, as mentioned, make people's working lives a grind, warp their personalities, perpetuate their ignorance, repress their spontaneity*

---

[128] Schmidt, Jeff, *Disciplined Minds: A Critical Look at Salaried Professionals and the Soul-battering System That Shapes Their Lives*, Rowman & Littlefield Publishers, 2001.

and stunt their personal development, amounting to a
kind of violence; those pushed over the edge tend to
"go crazy" in a particular way, aiming their guns up
the hierarchy more often than down.

The dominance hierarchy delivers violence but also manages violence. It encourages violence in divide-and-conquer schemes. It uses physical violence against the lower classes and the undesirables. But it disallows all violence that it does not originate or condone, even violence of thought, within the pacified middle and professional classes. It wants its subjects to be personally ignorant about conflict and about emotions related to conflict. "Hate" is not an allowed emotion. All the "ism" must be washed out, "whitewashed" as it were.

The underlying truth about the worker's condition, for the worker in any class, is that the barrier to meaningful self-fulfilment is hierarchical control, that this control makes one physically sick, and that liberation passes through identifying the real boss as the enemy and fighting against one's own oppression. Here the emotion of hate is as appropriate as one feels it for as long as one feels it. Here racism of self-defence against one's oppressor, if the power oppression is race-based, is as appropriate as one feels it for as long as one feels it. And so on.

The bosses don't want their hate and racism of oppression to generate the same emotions among their subjects, as driving forces for self-defence. So they engineer such reactions out of us. They pacify us, while continuing to violently oppress us.

If the boss is already providing an anti-racism policy then your far-reaching racism complaint is obviously out of whack. And any racist feeling you might have against whites is completely unacceptable. The boss' policy works in both directions in that it excludes all racism, black towards white and white towards black.

Well, any policy allegedly aimed at solving oppression but that "works in both directions" equally, on both the oppressor and the oppressed, ought to tell us something. Any such contract is nonsense and can only be about something else. This kind of "equality" maintains inequality, as surely as the law that both rich and poor equally cannot sleep under bridges.

The answer against the boss's real violence is not to eliminate all that the boss calls "violence", which is nonsensical and can only work in a group that is entirely willingly assimilated into service, but rather to use the necessary "violence" of self-defence against the true oppressor. No matter the form of the protest, the bosses will call it "violent", and it should be "violent" enough (i.e., determined enough) to succeed.

Likewise, the answer against workplace racism is not to eliminate all that the racist bosses call "racist", but rather to use the necessary "racism" of self-defence against the racist bosses and their representatives. No matter the form of the protest, the racist bosses will call it "racist", and it should be "racist" enough to succeed.

5. Institutions construct and maintain an illusion of the subject's personal responsibility for or of no causal responsibility for the subject's ailments arising from the institution's oppression.

On the health front, as I have explained above, the dominance hierarchy, via its leading impact on the immune system and vital body functions, makes subjects physically ill and is the leading causal factor of poor health. The system's response is two-fold. First, a main culprit (cancer) is alleged to be essentially random and to be solvable by the system's elite medical research (another alleged benefit of hierarchy). Second, the rest is alleged to be the subject's own fault in terms of diet and lifestyle choices.

In terms of meaningful relationships and meaningful work, the dominance hierarchy by design assures an absence of both, and carefully manages an illusion of what a normal relationship is, while providing all the chemical and substitute solutions needed to keep us in our places in futile lives.

The dominance hierarchy causes our defects, yet our defects are turned on us as proof of our defectiveness which, the system advances, must be the cause of all our ailments. I agree with the right to get off our butts, but to fight back—not to work harder under an assumption of a level playing field.

Similarly, institutional anti-racism solutions to racism are an illusion. Solving racism with institutional anti-racism hiring and behavioural proscriptions is analogous to solving the military's toxic and radioactive waste mega-problem, arguably the chief environmental disaster on the North American continent, not to mention post-war zones and military bases around the world, by introducing glass and paper recycling programs in middle-class neighbourhoods, in government offices, and on military bases.

Or, solving corporate and finance global predation by adopting ethical shopping and personal investment practices. If we all just did our part, as prescribed by the government and the experts then the "economy" would be forced to adapt to our choices and would become humane....

It would just be so comforting if our improved personal ethics could somehow impact vicious state, finance, and corporate practices against those less fortunate; if purifying our thoughts and cleansing our middle-class work environments could change the world....

This is all based on the crazy notion (since it is not supported by evidence) that top-down middle-class social engineering and language policing has a desirable impact on the widespread racism practiced under extreme power asymmetries. I argue that we should practice being powerful adults rather than seek paternalistic protections.

6. Institutions construct and maintain an illusion of optimized freedom in order to mask the oppression of its subjects.

Institutions expend considerable resources to convince us that the diminishing amount of our freedoms is the optimal balance between total freedom and the chaos that would unfurl if the institutions did not control our lives. Total freedom is presented as an unreasonable excess that would lead to deviance. We are made to understand that, just as we need stop signs and traffic lights, we need the bosses to optimize our productivity or the entire economy will come crashing down on our heads.

We are told that if we did not accept the imposed constraints, then society would stop to function because we would be taken over by aggressive competitors in a savage global economy.

We are told that we have freedom to work as hard as we wish in order to succeed, and that success is a direct consequence of our efforts. We are made to understand the logic of the corporate ladder and of promotions, bonuses, and earned benefits. Or, simply threatened with loss of job. We have the freedom to search for work elsewhere.

Our "own" politicians explain that their goal, for our good, is to attract investors to come and make work for us. Not so long ago, workers understood what an "investor" was. Now, thanks to the constant propaganda, we cheer on bought-and-paid-for politicians who sell the furniture in order to "attract investors", rather than make and take our own businesses and turf investors.

7. Individual freedom of expression is always a liability for institutions and is therefore always suppressed.

Of course, if individuals are free to say what they want, then propaganda loses its primacy. The boss' wise words are decoded and undone, as quickly as they are generated. Personal grievances become known rather than covered up, and we have interactions rather than coherent obedience.

Freedom of expression includes the freedom to not keep the boss's secrets. Such freedom is so rare that it is described as the rare phenomenon of whistleblowing. The penalties for whistleblowing are so immediate and severe that whistleblower legislation needs to be enacted in order to give a false façade of fairness for the most egregious cases of exposed boss "misbehaviours". Here, a boss's misbehaviour that can be acknowledged when exposed as a misbehaviour that significantly deteriorates one or more of the broad illusions used to control subjects.

Secrecy is an essential ingredient of control. Another essential ingredient is credibility and reputation of the boss, or the illusion of the boss's superiority in power, strength, judgement, knowledge, intelligence, and so on. A third essential ingredient is ignorance of the subjects, including ignorance about themselves. All these essential ingredients to a power structure are fundamentally threatened by freedom of expression. That's one freedom that needs to be very tightly constrained.

Expression can have a character which is predominantly political, such as a daring disclosure of a system's secret, predominantly to build ties, such as discussions leading to mutual support in the face of a common oppression, or predominantly to express a personal grievance or discomfort, such as an angry outburst intended to modify a colleague's behaviour, and so on. There are many dimensions to personal expression. All are needed because expression is both our influence on the outside world and our information about the outside world. If expression is constrained by the dominance hierarchy, then all facets of personal and community development are impacted and our existence is moulded and defined by hierarchy. The stronger the hierarchy, the more removed we become from our human nature.

The hate and racism of individuals, which are temporary emotional states or states of personal perception, must be distinguished from the hate and racism of the dominance hierarchy, which are permanent systemic features of hierarchical oppression. There is no reason, based on evidence, to believe that a cosmetic attack against visible hate and racism of the individual can lessen the system's hate and racism which generates the individual reactions to oppression.

Such engineered cosmetic approaches are displacements guaranteed to be ineffective. They are classic displacements engineered by the system. They include the above mentioned medical establishment proscriptions for healthy living, the ethical investment and consumption religions, and so on. It is a universally applied trick of the dominance hierarchy to divert attention away from the possibility of individually attacking systemic causes, and towards compliant behaviours of subjects, as mock solutions.

The "original sin" message, as always, is that the subjects are victims of their own defective characters, not victims of a vicious dominance hierarchy. The impacts of the dominance hierarchy on individuals are presented as evidence of the defective characters, which are not given an opportunity to repair via the needed praxis and free expression.

The only real solution is for individuals to break the cycle by directly confronting their own oppressions, which can only be realistically perceived through praxis which, in turn, includes free expression.

Similarly to hate and racism, "free expression" of the individual must be understood to be categorically different from "free expression" of the control hierarchy. While we must oppose all hierarchical communication which harms us, and make every attempt to disarm the dominance hierarchy, we should not allow the state to practice expression censorship against individual subjects.

The "free expression" of commands and directives[129] must be questioned, in resisting runaway hierarchy, but there is no moral basis for the state to limit individual expression among interacting individuals.

The fact that individuals have different degrees of racial status attributed by the hierarchy, such as white males, does not justify state

---

[129] Expression anchored in and wielding hierarchical power is not "free expression".

control of individual expressive interactions, nor can state control be of any practical value here. The individuals must work this out and they do when they decide to do so. There is no healthy substitute for this working out and it takes many creative forms, adapted to the hierarchical circumstances, including pink saris and bamboo sticks[130].

If you are perfecting the master's tools, then you are working for the master. One can use the master's tools against the master but when one does, the master does not comply.

---

[130] *Gulabi Gang—Rural women in pink saris, wielding bamboo sticks in pursuit of justice,* http://www.gulabigang.in/

Denis G. Rancourt

Free Expression, Basic Rights, and Abolitionism

THE "JUSTICE" SYSTEM'S treatment of basic rights is a brilliant example of how the hierarchy re-defines reality to suit its design. It is our incapacity, from being integrated, to have an allergic reaction to the nonsense of institutional language that allows legalese to enjoy its present status without being mobbed out of town.

Regarding basic rights, there is a general and pervasive legal "argument" that is an obscene muddle intended on the face of it to project paternalism and authoritarian control over people's lives: The accepted notion that one's individual rights are limited by infringement of the rights of others, as judged by the legal apparatus.

It would be interesting to review the history of this concept of rights being limited by the rights of others, no doubt first put forth by some illustrious academic service intellectual (renowned philosopher).

How could such hogwash have passed for authentic ethical reasoning? How could it have been sucked up so organically by the entire legal establishment? The answer is that it conveniently negates the concept of individual rights, while superficially appearing – in the logic of life in a dominance hierarchy—as though it preserves individual rights.

You have a right to life. When would your right to life interfere with the rights of others? In which circumstances would you need to be killed in order to preserve the rights of others? Given a high probability that you will kill others and as evaluated by whom? No. Your right to life is absolute. It does not interfere with the rights to life of others but your actual attempt to kill another does and is a crime which can be stopped and punished. But the punishment cannot violate your individual rights. A right is a right is a right or it is nothing.

You have a right to free expression. This right never negates the rights of free expression of others. If you are screaming loudly to prevent another from being heard you are both expressing yourself and preventing another from doing so. From a natural justice perspective, the first is absolutely protected whereas the latter is inadmissible and can be stopped and punished. But the punishment cannot violate individual rights.

If you are an army general and you give an order to commit a war crime then you are both expressing yourself and committing a war crime. The first is absolutely protected but the latter can legitimately be stopped and punished.

Just punishment is justice, not a violation of the criminal's rights. A punishment cannot be a violation of a criminal's rights. The general can be demoted and discharged, and forced to provide reparation, but his/her right to life and his/her freedoms of expression, association, and movement must not be violated beyond the negotiated requirements of reparation.

Social status and class and hierarchical status are not rights and can be removed as punishments. Mass or disproportionate accumulation of wealth and power is not a right. Likewise, you have no right to hide your crimes from public knowledge (which is the apparent purpose of so-called "transparency laws").

However, freedom of movement and association are fundamental rights. Prisons are illegitimate violations of individual rights and negate the possibility of reparation and rehabilitation.

Personal property ownership for personal use or need is a right.

Reparation for theft is immediate and need not involve negating rights. The thief keeps his/her right to personal property but must repair the damage caused and does not keep the illegally acquired property. Harm to persons is the reference.

Weapons are allowed for defence but cannot be used offensively. Rebellion is defence against an illegitimate master.

And so on. There is no need ever for a system to violate individual rights. The notion that criminals surrender their rights is barbaric, as barbaric as any slavery. Both only arise in hierarchical societies, which are always violently oppressive. Who decides what is a crime and what is a "just" punishment? Who decides who is a slave and what slavery entails? Where there will be war, extermination, lay-offs, and investments...?

The prison system is a system of mass torture and mass violations of human rights. It is a systemic symbol of hatred of humankind and a testament to a very sick society. The existence of a few pathological serial killers on the planet—made by the hierarchy that we inhabit—cannot begin to justify the crime against humanity that is the modern prison and segregation system.

And the entire genocidal prison system is enabled by exactly the kind of "brilliant legal mind" madness that is the concept that individual rights are constrained by the individual rights of others, as judged by the system. This logic relativizes rights thereby negating them and simultaneously wrongly justifies removing the rights of criminals.

Rights are rights. Wrong is wrong. Lawyers and judges are sick; as sick as a society with prisons and that practices genocide. There is no need for the obvious class and racial analysis of the prison population to assert the latter conclusion.

Name a single totalitarian or warring state, or any state, where the judges did not condone virtually everything that the state did. When have judicial rulings significantly impeded the advances of power's ambitions, on the basis of human rights? That's not their job.

Now that I have gotten it out viscerally, allow me to explain the point further. The concept of a human right of the individual cannot be discussed without a substantive consideration of the hierarchical reality. As soon as an individual is imbedded into a dominance hierarchy, the individual's basic rights are necessarily violated and the resulting tension must be managed by the oppressing system. This management is the system's full-time job and is accomplished by its institutions.

Consequently, the "justice" system, from government enacting laws to judges and lawyers to enforcement and confinement, is exactly meant to ensure a sustained and general negation of individual rights. It "makes sense" only in a world view that accepts hierarchical oppression and where the individual is primarily concerned with being oppressed fairly: "I pay my dues and others must do the same".

The system's underlying premise about rights is that rights are attributed according to social status, according to class, which in turn is determined or influenced by race, gender, and so on. From the very moment you interact with an institution—police intervention, walk into a courtroom, enter a school or hospital, apply for a job, pass security at an airport—it is clear what your rights actually are, as determined by your social class.

Many individual complaints about violated rights are actually complaints about having one's class status misattributed by an institution due to one's race, gender, etc. A main pseudo-right that is of major concern to integrated individuals is the "right" to access a higher class, the "right to education", the "right to just selection criteria", and so on. The latter are rights only to the extent that socio-economic stratification imposed by the dominance hierarchy is unjustified.

It is not an accident that the media give far more attention and credence to liberal middle-class rights activism about racial profiling than about racial socio-economic segregation. The first is a patch on a working dominance hierarchy, whereas the latter would be incongruent with the control imagery generated by the system. Police will be "educated" about racial profiling, as needed to appease criticism (i.e., intra-class unease), but the job of police to maintain socio-economic segregation or asymmetry is fully preserved.

Slavery was legal. Socio-economic segregation is legal. Prisons are legal. Global and domestic economic predations are legal. A nation's warring is legal, within national laws.

Final Thoughts

THE COLONIZER ROBS the victim even of the victim's racism against the colonizer. Integration of subjects who are not segregated or exterminated must be complete. The controller dispossesses the workers of their talk and of their personal fights in order to align them and keep them ignorant of themselves and dependent.

To go further, in the "civilized" dominance of "democratic" states, the master deprives the slave even of the master's opinion of the slave. That is, the bosses feign love towards the subjects, thereby completely robbing the subjects of all dignity. Malcolm X expressed his preference for straight talk from the oppressor this way[131]:

> *They don't stand for anything different in South Africa than America stands for. The only difference is over there they preach as well as practice apartheid. America preaches freedom and practices slavery. America preaches integration and practices segregation. Verwoerd is an honest white man. So are the Barnetts, Faubuses, Eastlands and Rockwells.*

---

[131] Malcolm X, Alex Haley, Playboy Interview, *Playboy Magazine*, May, 1963.
http://www.malcolm-x.org/docs/int_playb.htm

> *They want to keep all white people white. And we want to keep all black people black. As between the racists and the integrationists, I highly prefer the racists. I'd rather walk among rattlesnakes, whose constant rattle warns me where they are, than among those Northern snakes who grin and make you forget you're still in a snake pit.*
>
> [...]
>
> *The fact that I prefer the candor of the Southern segregationist to the hypocrisy of the Northern integrationist doesn't alter the basic immorality of white supremacy. A devil is still a devil whether he wears a bed sheet or a Brooks Brothers suit.*

Yet another appeal for free expression (here, across a hierarchical divide) from someone who knew the battle ground....

Obedient black university professors are not about to make revolution, any more than obedient white university professors. Both colours of service intellectuals serve. Anti-racism policy developed for the middle class citizenry of the World's most powerful state and its satellites is a social engineering tool to pacify the oppressed. We can add it to a large existing array of tools that includes: institutional religion, violence-induced despair, promise of reward-participation-integration, material compensation, entertainment, mood altering substances, prisons, hospitals, reserves, education, work, mass media, volunteerism, and so on. Many of the underlying organizations are beneficial to the individual when the organizational entity is self-managed or self-administered but are instruments of control in the hands of the dominance hierarchy.

As Paulo Freire would say, the only way to fight oppression is to fight one's own oppression. Since we all have the same oppressor, this can only bring us together. And only this fight can inform us about the true nature of the hierarchy, of our relation to it, and, therefore, of ourselves.

Hierarchy and Free Expression in the Fight Against Racism

In this struggle, Paulo urged us to not become the oppressor, by acting out of an authentic impulse for rebellion and liberation, rather than being moved by a will to gain a higher place in a dominance hierarchy[132]:

> *Freedom is acquired by conquest, not by gift. It must be pursued constantly and responsibly. Freedom is not an ideal located outside of man; nor is it an idea which becomes myth. It is rather the indispensable condition for the quest for human completion.*
>
> *[Otherwise, the participants] aspire to revolution as a means of domination, rather than as a road to liberation.*

In continually striving towards the ideal, individual rights must be held to be absolute, rather than attributable according to social status. This implies abolitionism, which is synonymous with dissolution of hierarchy[133].

---

[132] Freire, Paulo, *Pedagogy of the Oppressed*, 1970; Continuum, NY, 2000.

[133] *Denis Rancourt on anti-hierarchy activism*, Nine-part YouTube video miniseries, 2010.
http://activistteacher.blogspot.ca/2010/09/denis-rancourt-on-anti-hierarchy.html

Denis G. Rancourt

References Used

Breggin, Peter, *Brain-Disabling Treatments in Psychiatry*, 2008; http://www.breggin.com/

Breggin, Peter, *Toxic Psychiatry*, 1991; http://www.breggin.com/

Breggin, Peter, *The Violence Initiative*, video of conference talk, 2010; http://youtu.be/MQZdUmxG1Es

Churchill, Ward, *Pacifism as Pathology*, 1986.

Cleage, Rev. Albert, *Myths about Malcolm X*, speech delivered in Detroit, February 24, 1967

Climate Guy blog. http://climateguy.blogspot.ca/

Cockburn, Neco, *'Ambush' caused judge to withdraw from 'House Negro' civil suit, lawyers say*, July 27, 2012, *Ottawa Citizen*.

Darwin, Charles, *The Expression of the Emotions in Man and Animals*, 1872.

Farber, Jerry, *The Student as Nigger*, Contact Books, 1969.

Finkelstein, Norman G., *Resolving the Israel-Palestine Conflict: What We can Learn from Gandhi*, 2009.

Foner, Philip S. (Editor), *Mother Jones Speaks*, Monad Press, NY, 1983

France, Anatole, *Le Lys rouge*, 1894.

Freedman, David H., *Damned Lies, and Medical Science*, The Atlantic, 2010;
http://www.theatlantic.com/magazine/archive/2010/11/lies-damned-lies-and-medical-science/308269

Freire, Paulo, *Pedagogy of the Oppressed*, 1970; Continuum, NY, 2000.

Gates, Henry Jouis Jr., *Critical Race Theory and Freedom of Speech*, Chapter Five in "The Future of Academic Freedom", Menard, Louis, Ed., University of Chicago Press, 1996.

Gelderloos, Peter, *How Nonviolence Protects The State*, 2007.

Goffman, Erving, *Cooling the Mark Out: Some Aspects of Adaptation to Failure*, Psychiatry Vol. XV: 451-63. 1952.

Graedon, J. and Graedon, T., *Top Screwups Doctors Make and How to Avoid Them*, 2012, Three Rivers Press.

Gramsci, Antonio, *Letter from Prison* (19 December 1929).

Grignon, Paul, *Money as Debt*,
http://video.google.ca/videoplay?docid=5352106773770802849

Guevara, Che, *Guerrilla Warfare*, 1961.

Gulabi Gang, *Rural women in pink saris, wielding bamboo sticks in pursuit of justice,* http://www.gulabigang.in/

Haley, Alex, *The autobiography of Malcolm X,* Random House, 1964; Chapter 14.
http://autobiography-of-malcolm-x.wikispaces.com/14_black_muslims

Ioannidis, John PA, *Why Most Published Research Findings Are False,* 2005, PLoS Med 2(8): e124.
doi:10.1371/journal.pmed.0020124

Ioannidis, John PA *et al.,* *Replication validity of genetic association studies,* Nature genetics, 2001, 29(3), 306-309.

Ioannidis, John PA, *Contradicted and initially stronger effects in highly cited clinical research,* JAMA: the Journal of the American Medical Association, 2005, 294 (2), 218-228.

Jay, Dru Oja, *Questioning Climate Politics—Denis Rancourt says the 'global warming myth' is part of the problem,* April 11, 2007, interview in The Dominion.
http://www.dominionpaper.ca/articles/1110

Jones, Mary (Mother), Speech in Memorial Hall, Toledo, March 24, 1903. In: *Mother Jones Speaks,* Edited by Philip S. Foner, Monad Press, NY, 1983, p.98.

King, Martin Luther, *Why I Am Opposed to the War in Vietnam,*
YouTube video of sermon, Sermon at the Ebenezer Baptist Church on April 30, 1967. http://youtu.be/b80Bsw0UG-U

Kropotkin, Peter, *An Appeal to the Young,* 1880;
http://dwardmac.pitzer.edu/anarchist_archives/kropotkin/appealt

oyoung.html

Matsuda, Mari, Lawrence, Charles R. III, and Delgado, Richard, *Words that Wound: Critical Race Theory, Assaultive Speech, and the First Amendment*, Westview Press, Boulder, Colo., 1993.

Noble, David F., *Progress Without People*, Between The Lines, 1995.

Noble, David F., *Forces of Production: A Social History of Industrial Automation*, Oxford University Press, 1984.

Noble, David, F., *The Corporate Climate Coup*, 2007; http://activistteacher.blogspot.ca/2007/05/dgr-in-my-article-entitled-global.html

Parenti, Michael, *Blackshirts and Reds: Rational Fascism and the Overthrow of Communism*, 1997, City Lights Books.

Rancière, Jacques, *The Ignorant Schoolmaster*, 1991.

Rancourt, Denis G., *A Theory of Chronic Pain—a social and evolutionary theory of human disease and chronic pain*, Activist Teacher, December 20, 2011.

Rancourt, Denis G., *Academic Squatting: A democratic method of curriculum development*, Our Schools Our Selves, V. 16 N. 3 (#87) Spring 2007, p. 105-109.

Rancourt, Denis G., *The Activist Wars*, 2009.

Rancourt, Denis, G., *'Anti-racism' in support of racism*, Activist Teacher blog, 2011.
http://activistteacher.blogspot.ca/2011/10/anti-racism-in-support-of-racism.html

Rancourt, Denis G., *Anti-smoking culture is harmful to health—On the truth problem of public health management*, 2011; http://activistteacher.blogspot.com/2011/04/anti-smoking-culture-is-harmful-to.html

Rancourt, Denis G., *Canadian Education as an Impetus towards Fascism*, 2009 vol.1 issue.2 of JASTE (*Journal for Activist Science & Technology Education*), pages 68-77.

Rancourt, Denis G., *Collective intelligence does not imply individual intelligence—Technology does not come from geniuses*, 2011; http://activistteacher.blogspot.com/2011/11/collective-intelligence-does-not-imply.html

Rancourt, Denis G., *Critical race theory, in the service of whitey*, Activist Teacher blog, 2011. http://activistteacher.blogspot.ca/2011/08/critical-race-theory-in-service-of.html

Rancourt, Denis G., *Denis Rancourt on anti-hierarchy activism*, Nine-part video mini-series, 2010; http://activistteacher.blogspot.ca/2010/09/denis-rancourt-on-anti-hierarchy.html

Rancourt, Denis G., *Did Professor Joanne St. Lewis act as Allan Rock's house negro?*, U of O Watch, February 11, 2011. http://uofowatch.blogspot.ca/2011/02/did-professor-joanne-st-lewis-act-as.html

Rancourt, Denis G., *Global Warming: Truth or Dare?*, 2007. http://activistteacher.blogspot.ca/2007/02/global-warming-truth-or-dare.html

Rancourt, Denis G., *Gradual change is not progress*, Global Research, May 3, 2006.

Rancourt, Denis G., *How anti-racism protects class structure and dominance hierarchy*, Activist Teacher, 2011.
http://activistteacher.blogspot.com/2011/04/how-anti-racism-protects-class.html

Rancourt, Denis G., *Institutions build hierarchy between politico-cultural re-normalizations,* 2011;
http://activistteacher.blogspot.com/2011/11/institutions-build-hierarchy-between.html

Rancourt, Denis G., *Is establishment medicine an injurious scam?*, 2011;
http://activistteacher.blogspot.com/2011/11/is-establishment-medicine-injurious.html

Rancourt, Denis G., *Is the burning of fossil fuel a significant planetary activity?*, 2010.
http://activistteacher.blogspot.com/2010/08/is-burning-of-fossil-fuel-significant.html

Rancourt, Denis G., *Need for and Practice of Student Liberation*, essay, 2010.

Rancourt, Denis G., *On the gargantuan lie of climate change science*, Activist Teacher, March 21, 2011.
http://activistteacher.blogspot.ca/2011/03/on-gargantuan-lie-of-climate-change.html

Rancourt, Denis G., *On the racism and pathology of left progressive First-World activism*, 2010.

Rancourt, Denis G., *On the sociology of medical meta-science: Exposing*

the Truth supports the Lie, 2011.
http://activistteacher.blogspot.ca/2011/11/on-sociology-of-medical-meta-science.html

Rancourt, Denis G., *Radiation physics constraints on global warming: CO_2 increase has little effect*, on archive.org, December 3, 2011.
http://archive.org/details/RadiationPhysicsConstraintsOnGlobalWarmingCo2IncreaseHasLittleEffect

Rancourt, Denis G., *Rock Administration Prefers to Confuse 'Independent' with 'Internal' Rather Than Address Systemic Racism*, U of O Watch, December 6, 2008.
http://uofowatch.blogspot.ca/2008/12/rock-administration-prefers-to-confuse.html

Rancourt, Denis G., *Roundabout as conflict-avoidance versus Malcolm X's psychology of liberation*, essay, 2010.

Rancourt, Denis G., *Some big lies of science*, 2010.

Sapolsky, Robert M., *The influence of social hierarchy on primate health*, Review, Science, vol.308, p.648-652, 2005.
http://www.sciencemag.org/content/308/5722/648.abstract

Said, Edward, *Representations of the Intellectual*, 1994; Vintage Books, NY, 1996.

Schiermeier, Quirin, *Chemists poke holes in ozone theory: Reaction data of crucial chloride compounds called into question*, Nature 449, 382-383 (2007).
http://www.nature.com/news/2007/070924/full/449382a.html

Schmidt, Jeff, *Disciplined Minds: A critical look at salaried professionals and the soul-battering system that shapes their lives*, Rowman & Littlefield

Publishers, 2001.

Schrecker, Ellen W, *No Ivory Tower: McCarthyism & the Universities*, Oxford University Press, 1986.

Starfield, Dr. Barbara, *Is US Health Really the Best in the World?*, Journal of the American Medical Association, Vol.284, No.4, 2000, pages 483-485.]

Starfield, Dr. Barbara, *Health 'Care' in the United States*, interviewed on CHUO 89.1 FM Ottawa (Canada), The Train.

St. Lewis, Joanne, *Evaluation Report of Student Appeal Centre 2008 Annual Report*, November 15, 2008.
http://web5.uottawa.ca/admingov/documents/evaluation-report-sac-2008-annual-report.pdf

Student Appeal Centre (SAC), *Mistreatment of Students, Unfair Practices and Systemic Racism at the University of Ottawa*, Annual Report, November 2008, Student Federation University of Ottawa (SFUO).

X, Malcolm, *Message to the Grassroots*, speech, November 10, 1963, Detroit, Michigan.
http://www.sojust.net/speeches/malcolm_x_message.html

X, Malcolm, *My Philosophy is Black Nationalism* speech, Youtube:
http://youtu.be/Ix2-m1gDX8s

X, Malcolm, Haley, Alex, Playboy Interview, *Playboy Magazine*, May, 1963.
http://www.malcolm-x.org/docs/int_playb.htm

X, Malcolm, *The House Negro and the Field Negro*, YouTube video of a 1963(?) speech, http://youtu.be/znQe9nUKzvQ

Denis G. Rancourt

X, Malcolm, *The White Man Pays Reverend Martin Luther King*, YouTube
video of TV interview, http://youtu.be/nIdfVxCttZQ

About the Author

DENIS G. RANCOURT is a former tenured Full Professor of physics at the University of Ottawa in Canada. After receiving B.Sc. (University of Ottawa), M.Sc., and Ph.D. (University of Toronto) degrees in physics, and doing post-doctoral research under a Canadian scholarship in France and in The Netherlands, he was awarded a prestigious national Natural Science and Engineering Research Council of Canada university research fellowship, practiced several areas of science (including physics and environmental science), and ran an internationally recognized laboratory for twenty-three years. He was a regular invited, keynote, and plenary speaker at international scientific conferences in several areas of science and has published over one hundred articles in leading scientific journals. He taught thousands of university students, ran community outreach activities, developed popular activism courses, and was an outspoken critic of the university administration and a defender of student and human rights. He was fired for his dissidence in 2009 in what one expert observer called an "administrative mobbing" and in what is a major academic freedom case in Canada. He continues to write both science and non-science articles and to be a regular invited lecturer in a broad range of university courses.

His dismissal is before a binding labour tribunal with open court hearings which started in 2011 and are scheduled into 2013. During the hearings to date it was disclosed under oath and through document productions that he was the target of a broad covert surveillance campaign knowingly using a hired science student who adopted a false identity and gathered information that filled a wall-unit bookcase in the dean's office, in conjunction with the Legal Counsel of the university who is now a co-Chair (judge) of the Ontario Human Rights Tribunal. As part of the covert surveillance, his every web posting, talk, and media interview was recorded, transcribed, and commented on. His activities during holidays were reported, and so on.

Before he was fired—before he was even told that there was a recommendation that he be fired from his tenured position—he and his graduate students were locked out of their laboratory and student offices. His Research Associate of twelve years was summarily fired: she won a settlement after initiating a lawsuit. He was then banned from campus under university police escort. The University further had him arrested, handcuffed, and taken away when he attended the weekly Cinema Politica event that he created and had hosted for many years (all charges were later dropped by the prosecutor). He was barred from his weekly campus radio show. The arrest and campus ban were enforced by the former VP-Governance of the university who is now the General Counsel (director) of the Canadian Civil Liberties Association.

He continues to publish his *U of O Watch* blog, which he initiated in 2007. In 2011 a $1 million "private" defamation lawsuit was initiated against him, which he discovered through the courts is entirely funded by the University of Ottawa with no spending limit (according to sworn testimony), for a blogpost critical of a law professor and of the university president in their reaction to a student report alleging systemic racism at the institution.